Hoist a Cold One!

Historic Bars of the Southwest

Hoist a Cold One!

Historic Bars of the Southwest

Melody Groves photos by Myke Groves

University of New Mexico Press
Albuquerque

© 2011 by the University of New Mexico Press
All rights reserved. Published 2011
Printed in China by Oceanic Graphic Printing
16 15 14 13 12 11   1 2 3 4 5 6

Library of Congress Cataloging-in-Publication Data

Groves, Melody, 1952–
  Hoist a cold one! : historic bars of the Southwest / by Melody Groves and Myke Groves.
     p. cm.
  ISBN 978-0-8263-4668-1 (pbk. : alk. paper)
 1. Bars (Drinking establishments)—Southwestern States—History. 2. Bars (Drinking establishments)—Southwestern States—Pictorial works. I. Groves, Myke. II. Title.
  TX950.57.S85G76 2011
  647.9579—dc22
                              2010048820

Contents

Acknowledgments…vii

Introduction…1

Author's Note…5

Arizona

Bisbee Grand Saloon, Bisbee…9

Stock Exchange Saloon, Bisbee…13

Bird Cage Theatre, Tombstone…17

Crystal Palace Saloon, Tombstone…21

Golden Belle Saloon & Rawhide Steakhouse, Gila River Indian Community…25

Mayer Bar, Pioneer Living History Village, Phoenix…31

The Palace, Prescott…35

Colorado

Diamond Belle Saloon, Durango…43

Grumpy's Saloon, Silverton…47

Brown Bear Café, Silverton…51

Silver Eagle Saloon, Ouray…55

Black Jack's Saloon, Trinidad…59

Monte Cristo Saloon, Trinidad…65

New Mexico

Eklund Hotel, Clayton…71

Laguna Vista Lodge, Eagle Nest…75

Foster's Hotel, Chama…79

Express St. James Hotel, Cimarron…83

Los Ojos Restaurant and Saloon, Jemez Springs…89

Capitol Bar, Socorro…93

Owl Bar, San Antonio…97

Silver Dollar, Tinnie…101

The Lodge at Cloudcroft, Cloudcroft…105

Buckhorn Saloon, Pinos Altos…109

Double Eagle, La Mesilla…113

Texas

Rosa's Cantina, El Paso…121

Acknowledgments

Thanks to

Bert Clemens, Laguna Vista, Eagle Nest, New Mexico
Katie Clayton, the Palace, Prescott, Arizona
Rachel Howard, Bird Cage, Tombstone, Arizona
Loretta Day, Monte Cristo, Trinidad, Colorado
Mike Ryman, Monte Cristo, Trinidad, Colorado
Jerry Harrell, Double Eagle, La Mesilla, New Mexico
Buddy Ritter, Double Eagle, La Mesilla, New Mexico
Oscar Lopez, Rosa's Cantina, El Paso, Texas
Paula Manini, Trinidad History Museum, Trinidad, Colorado
Jane Besel, Carnegie Public Library, Trinidad, Colorado
Alice Romero, Carnegie Public Library, Trinidad, Colorado
Rod Timanus, Phoenix, Arizona
Karen Mazur, University of New Mexico Press, Albuquerque, New Mexico
Clark Whitehorn, University of New Mexico Press, Albuquerque, New Mexico
William Zerby, Woodcraft, Albuquerque, New Mexico

AND THANKS TO THESE FOLKS FOR CRITIQUING THE MANUSCRIPT:

Margaret Dean
Judith Avila
Sue Brown
Bart Cleveland
Phil Jackson
Peggy Spencer

Saloons, pubs, and taverns have been instrumental in shaping the West. A hub of social activity, saloons served as command central for information on issues ranging from elections to cattle drives.

Introduction

Giving up drinking is the easiest thing in the world. I know because I've done it thousands of times.
—Mark Twain

LIKE NOMADIC WOODEN GYPSIES, handmade mahogany, cherry, and oak bars traverse the world, surviving the ravages of both nature and man. It is truly the bars that are telling these stories as they make their way from saloon to saloon.

The quintessential western saloon sports a dimly lighted interior, the bar running lengthwise along the side as one enters. The bartender's handlebar mustache is as friendly as his handshake. The back bar, dark, heavily hand carved, often a Brunswick or perhaps a Sears, holds a wide variety of glasses and liquor. The front bar, a slab of wood complete with mustache rags and a brass foot rail, awaits elbows. The floor, dirt or rough wooden planks, hides under sawdust strewn around to absorb spills and to hold down the dust.

The story of Old West saloons and bars begins with the expansion of the West. All it took was one thirsty pioneer, and the rest . . . is history.

Before the United States headed west, as the Spanish explored and settled the region in the sixteenth century, the first watering holes were Mexican cantinas. However, the "holes" were few and far

Bars such as this one, in Tombstone's Bird Cage Saloon, anchor a room and serve as a focal point for socializing.

between. The first one called a saloon was Brown's Hole, in southern Wyoming, in 1822. Its clientele were fur trappers—the mountain men.

Saloons, pubs, and taverns have played a major role in shaping the United States. But there is more—a lot more—to saloons and drinking establishments than the proprietors, patrons, "working girls," and brew. And that is the bar itself. This wooden beauty anchors a room with its splendor, with the shining back bar towering over the bartender and the stable hardwood counter of the front bar. A fascinating variety of clientele have rested their elbows on these wonders while discussing anything and everything. More than a few policies and agreements have been decided here.

Saloons were not usually the largest buildings in western towns, but they were the most commonly used. Besides the obvious imbibing, they were the sites of judicial and social meetings. Judge Roy Bean held court in his own saloon in Langtry, Texas. The first church service at Hayes, Kansas, was held in a saloon. And Judge Amos Green conducted weddings as well as trials in his Socorro, New Mexico, establishment.

A saloon was, and still is, made up of three essential components: the back bar, the front bar, and the bartender.

Against the wall is the back bar—the cabinets, counter, and arched woodwork surrounding one or more mirrors—and it is what visitors notice first when entering. The back bar comes in three parts but when assembled appears seamless, a single piece of furniture. This is where the owner/proprietor displays the cornucopia of liquor, the bottle styles a large part of advertising a brand. The back bar also houses the magnificent large mirrors, those unfortunates that get broken when glassware, chairs, or people are thrown into them. The mirrors often post signs, some stern such as "Don't Ask for Credit," some not so much: "If You Spit on the Floor at Home, Spit on the Floor Here. We Want You to Feel at Home."

The central section of the back bar is a high altar of shining glassware. During the nineteenth and early twentieth centuries, bartenders would array assorted lemons, bottles of muscatel, and bottles of port along the back bar counter. No one called for these articles, but they were mentioned in the retail licenses—"wines and liquors"—and, as the millionaire columnist George Ade wrote, "they gave an air of aristocracy to a business venture terribly short on social standing."

The preferred spirits were rye in the eastern parts of the United States and bourbon in the South and West. Cocktails were requested sparingly. Veteran imbibers stuck to straight bourbon and rye, both of which were believed

A back bar consists of the arched woodwork surrounding one or more mirrors. More decorative than the front bar, it also holds bottles, the cash register, and glassware.

INTRODUCTION 2

effective in warding off effeminacy. In the sawdust saloons, those who had the courage to call for a Gin Daisy were simply asked to leave.

The whiskey served was wicked: water, with a touch of pure alcohol, molasses, tobacco juice, chilies, red pepper, and occasionally strychnine (its use was banned in Ohio in 1857) created Kansas Sheep Dip, Gut Warmer, Bug Juice, Taos Lightning, Tonsil Varnish, Redeye, Brave Maker, Tangleleg—the list goes on. Cactus Wine, made from a mixture of tequila and peyote tea, was also popular, as was Mule Skinner, made with whiskey and blackberry liquor. The house rotgut was often 100 proof, though it was sometimes cut by the barkeep with turpentine, ammonia, gun powder, or cayenne. Beer in Bisbee, Arizona, in 1867 ran ten to twelve cents a glass.

Beer in those days was never ice cold, usually served at 55 to 65 degrees. And it wasn't as sudsy as it is today. Patrons had to drink quickly, before it went flat or got too warm. However, some saloons stored huge chunks of ice (for example, Laguna Vista Saloon, with access to the nearby lake in Eagle Nest) in sawdust cellars, or used a high-falutin ice box (the Palace in Prescott, Arizona). But this all changed in the 1880s when Adolphus Busch introduced artificial refrigeration and pasteurization to the U.S. beer brewing process.

The front bar, the slab of mahogany, oak, or cherry, was where the men queued up, resting their elbows, shooting the breeze—or the bull. These were all "standing bars," meaning patrons stood at the bar to be served. This worked well, as this arrangement could fit in a large number of paying patrons. Many bars had spittoons or a trough on the floor, and most had mustache rags dangling underneath. These were communal rags for wiping froth from the patrons' mustaches. Health departments put a stop to them around

Beer, costing about ten cents a glass, was served at room temperature. Bourbon was the preferred drink in the West.

the 1950s, and spittoons were taken out during the great flu epidemic of 1918.

The bartender was essential to saloon life. A philosopher, an encyclopedia of sporting information, and a sympathetic humanitarian, he was always ready to head-wag appreciatively at the injustices of life or smile at rotten jokes. At least as long as the customer was still flush. Prototypical barmen slicked down their hair, displayed an expanse of

Bartenders of the Old West slicked down their hair, wore garters on their sleeves, and concocted a wide variety of cocktails.

gold watch chain, and wore a lodge emblem on a jacket of white, or once-white, duck.

A matter of professional pride among the barmen in fancy saloons was the ability to concoct some 150 different cocktails, rickeys, fizzes, cobblers, punches, and diverse "cups." But the staples remained beer and whiskey. Mostly the job consisted of pulling the tap or handling the bottle. If a rube came in, the bartender might switch out what was called the "cops' bottle"—the cheapest in the house.

In many saloons, tokens were used in place of coin change. When a man paid for his beer, whiskey, game of pool, or cigar and needed change, the proprietor gave him a token issued from his business. This would force the customer to come back to spend the token right there. Each saloon accepted only its own tokens, so if the customer came back, he would spend not only the token but, more than likely, buy other items as well. A game of pool cost two and a half cents, beer and cigars five cents. Some saloon tokens were good for a "smile"—a small whiskey. If the saloon owner was also the landlord of a brothel, the price was often negotiated.

Saloons also served practical needs: communication, social expression, a sense of belonging. They were warm and personal and "clubby."

Always inventive in time of need, men could lift a glass without benefit of a wooden building. For example, when a wagon train met a rail train, a bar was improvised out of doors. A wooden plank across two flour barrels served the mens' needs well. When a town was started, the first "buildings" to be erected were tent saloons. Saloons also floated aboard boats on the western rivers. Saloons were perhaps the first prefabricated construction: sections of buildings were moved out to railroad workers' railheads on flatcars and then set up quickly. In Forsyth, Montana, a temporary end of the line on the Northern Pacific Railroad, twelve saloons arrived in sections, each with the conventional bar, beer cooler, table, and piano. The bartender in one joint in Forsyth set out the drinks before the roof was on, with a professor spanking the ivories, and in a matter of hours a man had already been shot in an argument over a dance-hall girl.

Ah... the Old West. Good times...

Then the good times came to a halt. January 16, 1920, would stand out as a black day in bar history. Nationwide Prohibition began by federal constitutional amendment; however, some states, such as Arizona, had prohibited liquor sales years earlier. By January 17 the "alky" cookers were in business. While unregulated bootleg liquor remained abundant, the environment and flavor of the old-time saloon, the niceties of communal drinking, went underground.

It was not until 1933, when Prohibition was repealed, that saloons began to make a comeback. By then it was too late for many of the statuesque Brunswick and Sears bars; they had been hacked to pieces by Temperance fanatics or disappeared.

Surviving bars were turned into soda fountains, hidden in storage, or shipped to Mexico for safekeeping. Many never returned home. The ones that did preserve a fascinating history.

INTRODUCTION 4

Author's Note

INTRIGUED BY THE UNTOLD STORIES of the bars themselves, we decided to devote a book to the historic bars of the Southwest. What stories they tell! The buildings in which they are housed are themselves usually of great interest, but we focused on the wooden anchor of the saloon—the front and back bars.

Our search for historic bars took us to many interesting places, from the high deserts of Arizona and southern New Mexico to the mountains of Colorado and northern New Mexico. We especially looked forward to West Texas. Images of thirsty cowboys swinging open batwing doors and ordering a tall one were firmly fixed in our minds by countless Hollywood movies. Our hopes were dashed, however, as we searched Amarillo, Lubbock, and all points between. No saloons beckoned. No bars were to be found. It was in O'Donnell, Texas, childhood home of the actor Dan Blocker, where two gentlemen, curators at the town's museum, explained that this area is dry, always has been. There were no wooden bars because there were no saloons. No alcohol was sold. Ever. But "Grange meetings" out in somebody's barn or in a back alley where the white lightning flowed freely quite handily substituted on a Saturday night.

Returning to saloons and bars that still exist, a minor confession is in order. While three of the wooden bars were quite interesting, their antiquity and/or current serving status were not the sole reasons for including them in this book. It was "the place" that made the difference. Read about Rosa's Cantina in El Paso, Los Ojos in Jemez Springs, and the Bird Cage in Tombstone in the pages that follow.

This book celebrates the life and times, the miracle of survival, of these fascinating Old West bars. We hope you'll find opportunity to visit them yourself.

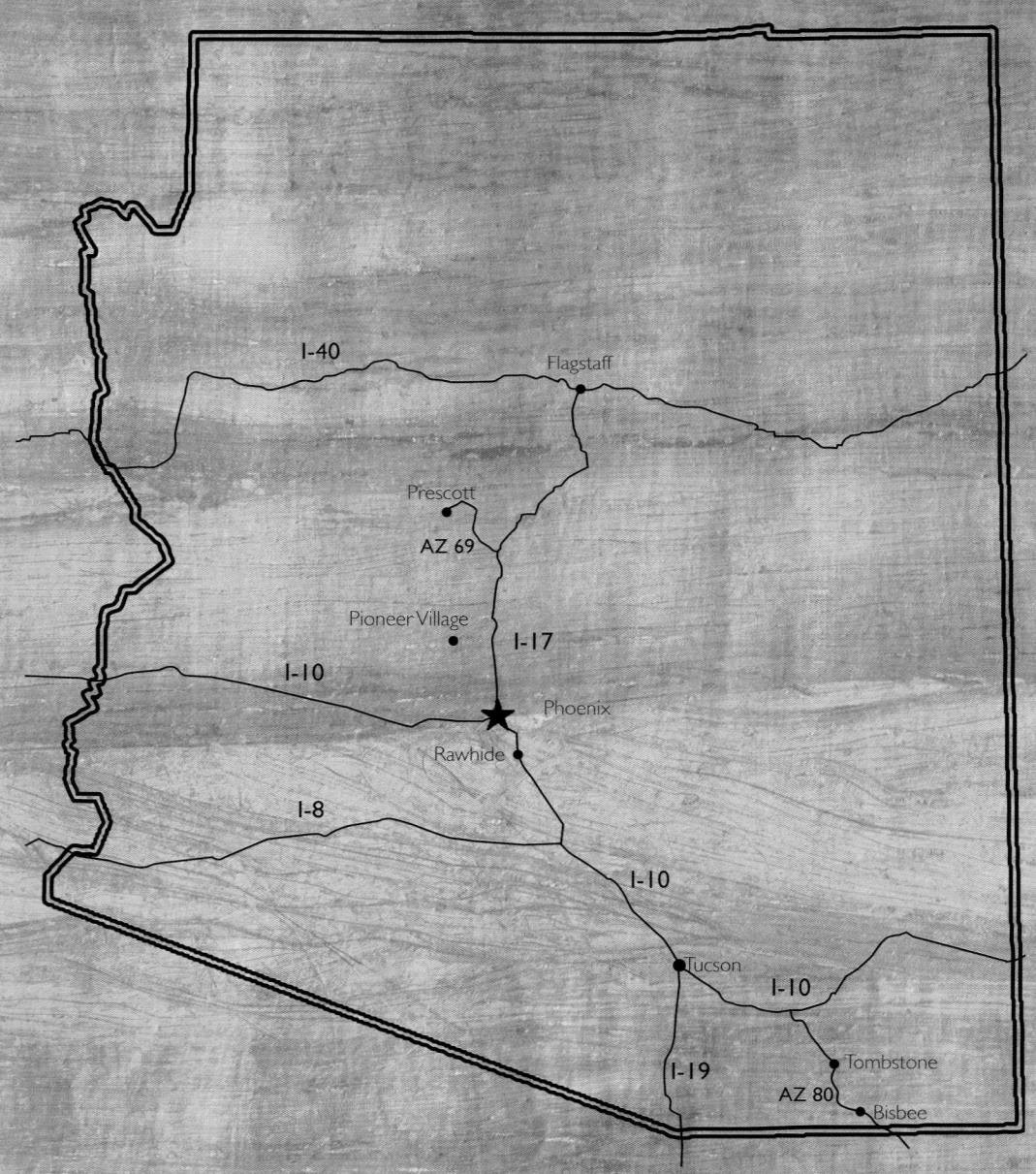

Arizona

Bartender Darlene Kaliher stands with history—an 1880s bar moved to Bisbee during the town's early 1900s heyday.

Bisbee Grand Saloon

BISBEE

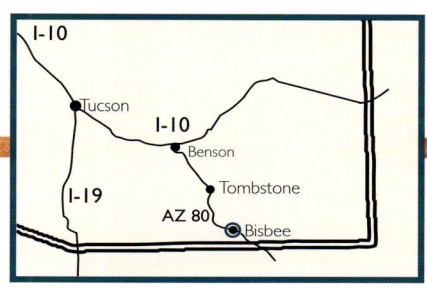

Here, we know everybody's name.
—Darlene Kaliher, bartender

Well built and set on solid rock, these 1890s buildings are still sound.

REMINISCENT OF THE WELCOMING ATMOSPHERE in television's hit show *Cheers*, the Bisbee Grand Saloon warms visitors, old and new alike. No one is a stranger for more than half a minute. This is the saloon where, quicker than it takes to order a drink, out-of-town visitors find themselves joking and laughing right along with the regulars.

The bartender, Darlene Kaliher, enthuses about the saloon, the hotel, the building, and, for that matter, the entire town of Bisbee. And not much gets past her. But what she does know best is everyone's name. She even knows the dogs' names when they come in and sit at their owners' feet. And the doggie biscuits are free of charge.

Dogs aside, one look at the back bar, and visitors know they have stepped into another world, a historical world. Kaliher explains that the 1880s back bar once graced the Pony Saloon in the famous town of Tombstone. The reason it moved thirty miles south is up for discussion, but it has sat in this Bisbee saloon since around 1906 when the front bar and hotel were built.

A fillet of intricate scrollwork adorns the top bar columns.

And since 1906 "people have come here to stay in touch," states Kaliher. A regular customer concurs. He explains that after work he hightails it to the Bisbee Grand Saloon where he sits and chats with fellow customers. A couple of times a month, the faculty of Cochise College in Bisbee comes in for a "reconnecting" session.

The Bisbee Grand Saloon caters to everyone, especially the locals. The Red Hat Ladies Society meets here. And not to be outdone by crimson chapeaux, a group of men wearing women's lingerie, locally called "the lingerie group," parades through in their red thongs and not much else. They visit most of the bars in town before going home. This spectacle happens in mid-August, when the weather is warm.

New Year's and Halloween crowds are repeat customers. However, the regulars report the best time to come is on Friday afternoons when the saloon dishes up a free buffet during happy hour. Local bands on weekends round out a full experience, and rest assured, Darlene *will* know your name before you walk out that door.

History

Bisbee is a living example of the early mining towns of Arizona; others grew quickly, then died just as fast. At 5,300 feet in the Mule Mountains, Bisbee is situated at the far southeastern corner of the state, close to the Mexican border, yet hidden in the mountains. Its moderate climate makes rose cultivation a prime avocation. Here Old West style mingles with brick Victorian buildings, creating a sense of survival through a century in which copper mining has become only a memory.

Getting There

Bisbee is 100 miles south of Tucson on U.S. Highway 80. The Bisbee Grand Saloon is at 61 Main Street; (800) 421–1909; www.bisbeegrandhotel.com.

opposite page, top left: Boots rest on a brass rail. The front bar, painted white, is set off with black and gold trim.

opposite page, lower left: The top of this Corinthian column shows off Greek design. Egg-and-dart molding runs along the top of the bar.

opposite page, top right: In 1880- Bisbee was named in honor of Judge DeWitt Bisbee, one of the financial backers of the adjacent Copper Queen Mine.

opposite page, middle right: Drawer pulls were highly ornate in early bars.

opposite page, bottom right: A rather wooden "local resident" resides over the bar.

right: Pressed tin ceilings, capped by copper moldings, are indicative of the era.

It's hard to hide a bar of this size in Mexico. But that's where it waited out Prohibition.

Stock Exchange Saloon

BISBEE

The Gulch is still alive today.
—Patricia Steward, owner

WHO WOULD HAVE THOUGHT that from 1880 through 1910 Bisbee, Arizona, would be the largest town west of the Mississippi River? A town where there was a saloon for every church? A town as wild and woolly as Tombstone? While this picturesque town today may be a shadow of its former self, it's still booming. In fact, it's an artist's paradise. This is where the past meets the future to create a mesmerizing present.

The Stock Exchange Saloon, built by John Muheim, opened in 1905 as the Brewery Saloon. Business boomed as copper, gold, silver, and other minerals were mined. The back bar, along with its service counter, originally graced a hotel in Douglas, Arizona. When it closed, the bar and counter were shipped to Bisbee on the El Paso & Southwestern Railroad.

Placed against the north wall, the bar and counter provided miners, ranchers, and even cattle rustlers with a place to lean as they mulled over the day with a shot of whiskey or homemade beer in hand. The gaiety was short-lived. Arizona celebrated statehood in 1912 and by 1914 had become a dry state, enacting Prohibition six years before the rest of the country. In 1914 the Brewery Saloon closed its doors. The back bar and service counter were disassembled and shipped to San Luis, Baja, Mexico. They met the fate of so many other bars during those Prohibition years.

Built by John Muheim, the Stock Exchange Saloon, formerly the Brewery Saloon, has not changed much since 1905.

By the early 1900s Bisbee was the largest city in the Southwest between St. Louis and San Francisco.

Because of the town's size and the amount of business, the brokerage firm of Dewey and Overlock moved their upstairs offices downstairs to the now-vacant saloon. A stock board was installed where the bar used to be, and a ticker tape was sent from the offices of E. F. Hutton in New York. The New York Stock Exchange in Arizona—the only one in the state—was born. In fact, it was the only stock exchange office in the West.

For fifty years the stock exchange office hummed with use. Then, in 1964, it closed. The huge board sat, figures and tallies not erased. Today the titles and companies listed on that board are the same ones listed the day the office closed.

Fast forward to 1980. The saloon, once again housing liquor and frivolity, opened its doors as the Stock Exchange Saloon. The original back bar and service counter were brought back from Mexico and placed along the south wall. A unique aspect of this saloon is the front bar—made from the stock exchange teller's cages. The long counter is divided by posts that support another beam overhead. It is said that a toy train ran along the top.

The owner, Patricia Steward, reports, "My saloon draws a lot of tourists, not only because of the building's history, but also because of the climate in Brewery Gulch along Tombstone Canyon. We have the finest year-round temperature in the world, always staying between 70 and 90 degrees." And if that isn't enough, everyone from old-timers to bikers favor the Stock Exchange Saloon.

History

Bisbee, Arizona, named for Judge DeWitt Bisbee of San Francisco, was founded in 1880 and today has 6,500 permanent residents. A city of refinement and culture, it boasted in its heyday a population of 25,000, including many miners and businessmen. Bisbee sits at the confluence of two canyons. Tombstone Canyon, later called Main Street, became the central business district. The other canyon, Brewery Gulch, blossomed into a raucous district full of saloons and shady ladies. Action slowed around 1910 when prostitution was outlawed. Prohibition sent thirsty patrons across the border to Naco, Mexico.

The mines closed in the mid-1970s, and the town fell into a depressed era, but within a decade artists discovered Bisbee and revitalized it.

Getting There

Bisbee is 100 miles south of Tucson on U.S. Highway 80. Exit at Tombstone Canyon and continue downhill about 3.5 miles to Brewery Avenue.
15 Brewery Ave.; (502) 432–1333; www.stockexchangesaloon.com.

opposite page: Beginning in 1914, when Arizona enacted Prohibition, the Brewery Saloon was turned into the only stock exchange in the West.

top right: Reopened in 1980, this saloon draws tourists who like to soak in history.

bottom right: The Stock Exchange greets visitors to Brewery Gulch.

Wyatt Earp and Doc Holliday leaned against this bar. Today it is Tombstone's only remaining bar of the 1880s in its original building. Note the "orb" captured in this photo at the bottom of the bar.

Bird Cage Theatre

TOMBSTONE

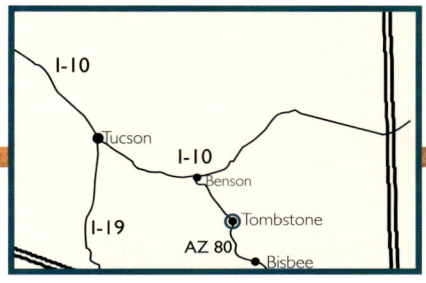

The ghosts saved our bar.
—Rachel Howard, building guide

STEP BACK TO 1881. Nothing but mines pockmarked the low, rambling hills of Tombstone, Arizona Territory. Everywhere one turned, another mineshaft burrowed into the ground like a prairie dog looking for sanctuary. With those mines came miners—thirsty, tired, looking-for-fun miners—many with money in their pockets.

Enter the scene, saloons and gambling parlors. There were plenty to separate the miners from their money. One such establishment stood out from all the rest. The Bird Cage Opera House and Theatre ("opera house" was used in an attempt to make it appear "respectable"), perched at the edge of the prostitution district, soon became the pinnacle of rowdy, bawdy, rootin-tootin', honky-tonk entertainment. In 1882 it drew the attention of the *New York Times*, which referred to it as "the wildest, wickedest night spot between Basin Street and the Barbary Coast." In nine years this den of "negotiable affections" operated twenty-four hours a day, seven days a week, housing the longest continuous poker game ever played—eight years, five months, and three days. The poker table still stands as it was left, complete with its chairs on the dirt floor.

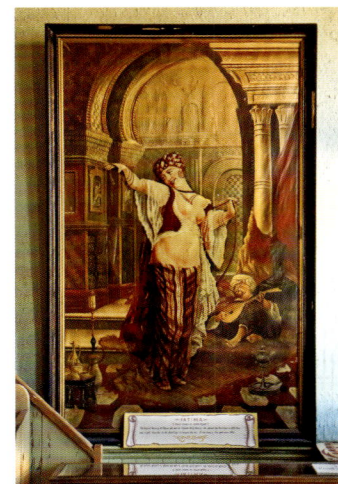

Little Egypt gave this poster to the Bird Cage in 1882. It carries six bullet holes and stands nine feet high.

The *New York Times* referred to the Bird Cage in 1882 as the "wildest, wickedest night spot between Basin Street and the Barbary Coast."

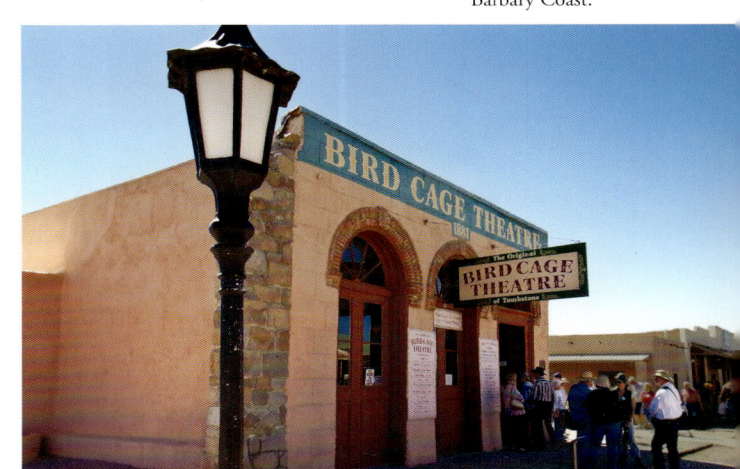

"Red-coated bartenders poured nothing but Tombstone's best," states the Bird Cage Theatre's brochure. And they poured it at the cherry bar, the only one still in its original location in all of southeastern Arizona. Built in Pittsburgh, Pennsylvania, this bar traveled across the Atlantic, around Cape Horn, and up the Pacific, finally arriving in San Francisco after a six-month trip. From there, bars usually went by rail to their destinations. However, the railroad would not insure the French mirrors of the bar destined for the Bird Cage, so the bar and mirrors were loaded onto a wagon train and hauled over mountains and deserts to Tombstone.

Over 140 holes riddle the walls and ceilings of the Bird Cage, some of them from the gunfights that occurred in the nine years it was open. This one is in a column of the front bar.

Billy Hutchinson, original owner of the Bird Cage, planned to situate the bar on the west wall of what is now the lobby. However, it was too tall. The back bar did not fit between the playbills as its height covered the catwalk, so Hutchinson turned it 90 degrees to the south wall, where it stands today. Originally, there were three doors facing east, one opening against the bar. Solution? Nail the door shut and create a window.

As was common in bars of the Victorian era, dentils, beading, and appliqué carving adorn the tops and sides of the bar at the Bird Cage.

Just who has leaned against that bar, ordering drinks, making plans, telling yarns? The list reads like a who's who of western characters. Wyatt Earp met his future wife, Josephine (Sadie) Marcus (of Neiman Marcus fame), here. Among the many others were Diamond Jim Brady, Curly Bill Brochius, Doc Holliday, John Clum, Big Nose Kate, Johnny Behan, Lily Langtree, Lotta Crabtree, Eddy Foy, Lillian Russell, Luke Short, the Clantons, the other Earp brothers—Virgil, Morgan, and James—Ethel Barrymore, businessmen Adolph Busch and George Randolph Hearst, and photographer C. S. Fly.

The Bird Cage was a gambling hall, saloon, theatre, and brothel, and no self-respecting woman in town would even walk on the same side of the street. It opened on Christmas Day 1881 and operated twenty-four hours a day, seven days a week, until it closed its doors in 1889. The ladies of the evening plied their trade in little crib-style compartments suspended from the ceiling. These ladies were the inspiration for the song "She's Just a Bird in a Gilded Cage," which was quite popular during the early 1900s.

Rowdy doesn't begin to describe the Bird Cage. Over 140 bullet holes are silent testaments to the high times. A .45 slug still lies buried in the front of the cherry wood bar.

It all came to a screeching halt in 1889 when the mines flooded. The owner simply shut off the lights and said, "I'll be back tomorrow." It would be more than forty years, in the 1930s, before it opened again, everything intact, just as he left it.

But not everything stayed the same. While the patrons moved on to another world, the Bird Cage developed a reputation for being haunted. Ask the people who work there. They'll tell you. In fact, beginning in the 1920s during Prohibition, Temperance Leaguers would peer through the windows at that beautiful bar and wield their axes, intent on destroying the center of vice in town. However, voices, honky-tonk music, singing, and card-shuffling noises coming from inside this vacant building kept the Temperance people out. No one was brave enough to enter such a haunted building. As Rachel Howard, one of the guides says, "The ghosts saved our bar." Whether you believe in ghosts or not, it makes a delicious story.

As a National Registered Landmark and Historic Landmark of the American West, the Bird Cage opened its doors again in 1934, not as a bawdy house, but as a sandwich shop. That business didn't last long. There is a fee to tour the building. However, access to the bar in the lobby is free.

Although it is no longer possible to belly up to the bar and order a drink, you can rest your elbows right where Bat Masterson did, right where Johnny Ringo did, right where Wyatt Earp did. Right where their ghosts still do.

History

Founded in 1877 by a prospector named Ed Schieffelin, Tombstone was named after his first mining claim, which produced silver. Prospectors, cowboys, homesteaders, lawyers, gunmen, and businessmen flocked to the booming town. In the mid-1880s the population reached 7,500, which includes only white male registered voters over the age of twenty-one. The actual population is estimated to have been closer to 20,000.

Tombstone's heyday saw over one hundred saloons, numerous restaurants, a thriving red-light district, a large Chinese district, schools, churches, newspapers, and the first public swimming pool in Arizona (still in use today). Fire raged through Tombstone in June 1881, taking more than sixty businesses with it. In May 1882, while the paint was still fresh on the new buildings, fire swept through again, destroying a large portion of the business district. The Bird Cage survived both fires, and the town again rebuilt.

The famous Shootout at the OK Corral on October 26, 1881, happened in just twenty-four seconds, with thirty shots fired. The Earp brothers, along with their family friend Doc Holliday, mortally wounded Billy Clanton and Tom and Frank McLaury. In the opinion of some people, it is the notoriety of this one brief, violent event that keeps Tombstone alive.

As the mines flooded, industry slowed, and the town died. In the early 1930s the population dwindled to 150. Today tourism and ranching are the mainstays of the approximately 1,500 residents.

Getting There

Tombstone is 35 miles south of Benson, Arizona. From I-10, take U.S. Highway 80, which becomes Freemont Street. Allen Street is one block to the west. The Bird Cage Theatre is at Sixth and Allen Streets; (520) 457–3421; www.amwest-travel.com.

top right: The original 1881 gaslight features have been converted to electricity.

middle right: Unusual in design, this top rail, with its brass support, provides a shelf for elbows.

bottom right: Made in either Austria or Germany, this 1880s Vienna Regulator clock specifies the day of the month with an indicator attached to the weight.

The hand-built Crystal Palace bar sets the scene for a good Saturday night of honky-tonking.

Crystal Palace Saloon

TOMBSTONE

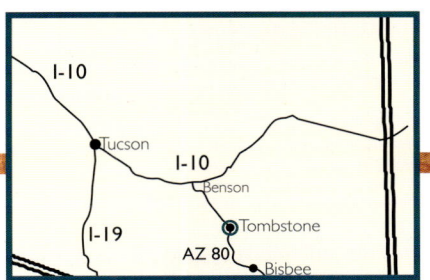

The most famous saloon in the West.
—Saloon motto

FIRST CAME SMOKE. Then fire. Then Prohibition. Then another fire. The huge mahogany bar in the Crystal Palace burned to the ground. Another bar was built, then placed in storage in Mexico, and then that building burned. Was it fate?

The Golden Eagle Brewery, the present-day Crystal Palace Saloon, has served as a cornerstone of Tombstone since 1879. Located on the corner of Fifth and Allen Streets, it has risen from the ashes—twice.

Back in the day, the Golden Eagle featured fine bock beer, free lunch, and a display of live wild animals. However, as with so many towns, fire swept through Tombstone on June 22, 1881. A local saloon owner pouring out a batch of bad whiskey dropped his cigar into it. Poof! Although much of the town burned to cinders, the Golden Eagle was saved by a large bucket brigade. The Brewery was singed but intact. However, less than a year later, on May 26, 1882, a fire totally destroyed the building, taking the saloon's front and back bars with it.

But you can't keep a good tavern down long, and on July 23, 1882, the Crystal Palace Saloon reopened its doors, rising out of the Eagle's ashes. The Crystal Palace became known for its fine dining, serving

Twice burned down, the Golden Eagle Brewery rose from the ashes and is now the Crystal Palace.

above: This applied carving is set off by beading and mahogany molding.

right: A Seth Thomas antique clock adorns one wall of the Crystal Palace.

oysters and other delicacies. Gambling and live music were part of the action. The Crystal Palace became the place most frequented by those individuals prominent on the business and social registers of Tombstone.

This building housed one of Tombstone's first saloons, with the brewing company located directly behind it. The Wehrfritz Building, named after it builder, was expanded by adding a second story. The offices of U.S. Deputy Marshal and Tombstone Marshal Virgil Earp and Dr. Goodfellow were there. "Buckskin" Frank Leslie was the night watchman.

And who frequented the Crystal Palace? Mine officials, gunmen, prospectors, rustlers, lawyers, stagecoach bandits, cowboys, lawmen, gamblers, homesteaders, and outlaws. Big Nose Kate, Doc Holliday's girlfriend, was rumored to have spent a great deal of time at the saloon.

Life was good, busy, and prosperous until Arizona enacted Prohibition in 1914 (prior to federal Prohibition) and put the skids on serving alcohol. Reportedly, a businessman purchased the roulette wheels, gaming tables, and mahogany front and back bars, along with other fixtures for his saloon in Naco, Mexico. Reports state that two years later a fire swept through *his* saloon, leaving nothing standing.

The Crystal Palace was not the only casualty of Prohibition. Several bars found themselves turned into soda fountains, or stored in Mexico, some in commercial buildings, some in warehouses, some under tarps, waiting for the

repeal of Prohibition, which finally came in 1933. A few bars made it home; many did not. Many have been lost.

Although the original bar at the Crystal Palace never made it back across the border, a replica was hand built in Tucson in 1964. Attention to detail, down to the last inch, is obvious. Historic Tombstone Adventures (HTA), an organization formed to preserve and restore many of the town's landmarks, purchased the Crystal Palace. After poring over old photographs and every available written record, HTA commissioned craftsmen to restore the Crystal Palace.

When you step inside, pause for a moment and consider its history. The original copper ceiling, the adobe walls, and the magnificent bar stand quietly, and you can hear Johnny Ringo and Doc Holliday debating about guns, Virgil and Wyatt Earp spinning a faro wheel, and Big Nose Kate laughing at their jokes.

History

The town of Tombstone was established in 1877 when Ed Schieffelin named the area after his first mining claim. The town boomed until the 1890s, when the mines flooded. Tombstone dwindled to just a few hardy souls, but "the Town Too Tough to Die" resurrected itself. A committee created Helldorado Days in a nod to the famous 1881 Shootout at the OK Corral. Tourists, Old West reenactors, and locals alike flock every October to experience the gunfights and see the "painted ladies" for a true taste of the Old West.

Getting There

Tombstone is 35 miles south of Benson, Arizona, on I-10. Take U.S. Highway 80, which becomes Freemont Street. Allen Street is one block to the west. The Crystal Palace Saloon is at 436 E. Allen Street; (520) 457–3611; www.crystalpalacesaloon.com.

top right: An American wheel, identified by the "oo"; European wheels use only one "o." *Roulette* means "little wheel" in French.

bottom right: The wooden boardwalks creak under boot steps, just like they did in the 1880s.

This acanthus leaf carving hides the center seam of the back bar.

23 & Crystal Palace Saloon

Cowboys, businessmen, tourists, and even Civil War and Old West reenactors stop in at the Golden Belle for a cold one.

Golden Belle Saloon & Rawhide Steakhouse

GILA RIVER INDIAN COMMUNITY

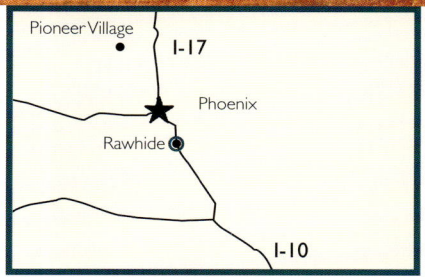

The West is still alive.
—Saloon motto

ENDURING MONTHS PENNED UP in a ship's cargo hold, a fine hand-carved French mahogany bar journeyed across the Atlantic Ocean in the early 1900s. From France to San Francisco, around Cape Horn, through perilous waters, then up the west coast of South and North America, the trip proved harrowing at best. When it finally landed in northern California, this magnificent bar was met by George Lewis "Tex" Rickard. He packed it onto wagons and hauled it by mule train over mountains, across rivers, and down to the new town of Goldfield, Nevada.

In 1902 gold was discovered, and the town of Goldfield sprang up. By 1904 the Goldfield district had produced eight hundred tons of ore, valued at $2.3 million—30 percent of the state's production that year. Goldfield boomed, becoming Nevada's largest town from 1903 to 1910. Between 1903 and 1940 Goldfield's mines produced ore worth more than $86 million.

It was here in 1904, in Tex Rickard's Northern Saloon, where the men first leaned over the French wooden bar, swapping yarns, ordering drinks,

above: A bridge crosses into the Old West amusement park that houses the Golden Belle Saloon.

below: Entry to the Golden Belle is free.

left: Starting life in France, this hand-carved beauty has traveled more than most people.

right: In 1884 John H. Patterson founded the National Cash Register Company, maker of the first mechanical cash registers.

discussing the ups and downs of mining. Times were good. The Northern was the most celebrated saloon and gambling house in the area. In fact, because of the saloon, Wyatt and Virgil Earp made their homes in Goldfield in 1904. Virgil was hired as deputy sheriff in January 1905. Wyatt had met Rickard in Nome, Alaska, where Rickard had opened a gambling hall. At Rickard's request Wyatt went to work for Rickard at his Goldfield establishment as a pit boss, an overseer of casino workers.

In October 1905 Virgil Earp died of pneumonia in Goldfield, with his wife, Allie, at his side. Shortly afterward Wyatt Earp left town.

Tiring of the area, Rickard sold his Northern Saloon, packed up the bar, and moved. He drove his 1907 Thomas Flyer to Rawhide, Nevada, and built another Northern Saloon with the money from his transaction. Once more, he set up his beautiful mahogany bar.

In Rawhide Rickard met and hired the boxer Jack Dempsey. Not only did Rickard promote Dempsey's boxing career but he also hired him as a bouncer for his saloon. It is reported that the Northern Saloon in Rawhide became so successful that hundreds of people were needed to run it. A devastating fire burned down the Northern in 1908, but somehow the bar was spared. Rickard chose not to rebuild and instead became a boxing promoter.

After decades of its whereabouts lost to time, the bar resurfaced and made its way down to Rawhide, Arizona. Patrons today still lean against the wood, rest their elbows, and order a cold one. Whose famous elbows have rested there? Virgil and Wyatt Earp for sure. Jack Dempsey, too. And modern-day Civil War and Old West reenactors.

Rawhide, Arizona's largest western-themed authentic frontier town attraction, moved from Scottsdale, Arizona, to Wild Horse Pass at the Gila River Indian Community a few years ago. Because of the attention to detail, it is easy to stand on the corner of this town and feel transported back a hundred years to the days when the West was new. For a theme park, it's mighty lifelike.

Step into the Golden Belle at the Rawhide Steakhouse and Saloon. Could this be the 1880s? It sure feels like it, except for the much-appreciated air-conditioning in the summer and the beer that is much colder than it would have been back then.

The saloon is saturated with history. The stained-glass domed entry is a perfect place to launch a tour of the amazing assortment of historical pieces the Golden Belle's owners have collected. The gold-framed mirror opposite the bar was purchased in France by William Randolph Hearst and was to be used at Hearst Castle in San Simeon, California. Later it was purchased by MGM studios and used in many of its motion pictures.

The beautiful brass chandeliers hanging in the saloon are from the Healy Hotel (later renamed the Earl), built in 1906 in Ogden, Utah, and razed in 1967. It was Utah's finest

bottom left: The capital shown here is decorated in Romanesque style.

right: Stepping into the Golden Belle launches patrons back in time. This stained-glass dome is one of a kind.

bottom right: Originally from Ogden, Utah's Healy Hotel, this brass chandelier now graces the Golden Belle.

This applied carving sits under classic egg-and-dart trim beading, gracing the back bar. Note the lion's head woodwork detail. The ornate chandelier is electric.

hotel and stood next to the Union Pacific Depot. Many other antiques adorn the steakhouse.

Tex Rickard

George Lewis "Tex" Rickard (1870–1929) was an American boxing promoter and the founder of the New York Rangers National Hockey League franchise. Part of the most famous of all three-way partnerships was that of Jack Dempsey, his manager, Jack Kearns, and Rickard. Together they grossed $8.4 million in only five fights between 1921 and 1927. They ushered in the golden age of professional boxing in the 1920s.

Rickard handled boxing's first $1 million gate (Dempsey vs. Carpentier in 1921), built Madison Square Garden in 1925, founded the New York Rangers as a Garden tenant in 1926, named the NHL team after himself (Tex's Rangers), and built the Boston Garden in 1928. During the 1920s Tex Rickard was the leading promoter of the day. He has been compared to P. T. Barnum and Don King.

History

Gila River Indian Community

The Maricopa Indians, who originally called themselves Pee Posh, settled with the Akimel O'odham tribe to share resources and space along the Gila River in central Arizona. Together they fought off the warring Apache and Yuman tribes.

In 1846 in southern Arizona, gold-crazed men trekked across the Sonoran Desert in search of the riches California held. As one of the primary routes to the goldfields between 1849 and 1851, the Sonoran Desert was crossed by an estimated sixty thousand travelers, many of them ill prepared for the harsh conditions. The Maricopa and Akimel O'odham tribes provided water, food, and shelter to the desperate men. Wrote Lt. Sylvester Mowry in 1857, "Their stores of wheat and corn have supplied many a starved emigrant, and restored his broken down animals."

In 1854 the Gadsden Purchase made southern Arizona officially part of U.S. territory, and in 1859 Congress established the first reservation in Arizona, encompassing 372,000 acres along the Gila River. Within three years the people on this reservation grew more than one million pounds of wheat, most of which was sold.

Having survived near-disastrous interactions with non-Natives, the Gila River Community is home to several businesses and entertainment establishments. According to the Community's website, "The natural elements of the environment have been embraced by our artisans in the form of artwork, pottery, baskets and jewelry. Even our buildings feature symbolic designs, natural materials and plants which reflect their affection for the land." The boundaries encompass 600 square miles.

Call ahead to verify operating hours.

Getting There

Rawhide, Arizona, is 15 miles south of Phoenix. The 1880s western theme park is located at the Gila River Indian Community. Except for special events, admission to the theme park is free, and it's always free for the Steakhouse and Golden Belle Saloon. From I-10, take Wild Horse Pass exit 162 west and follow the signs; (480) 502–5600; www.rawhide.com.

Old West reenactors bring the Mayer Bar to life.

Mayer Bar

PIONEER LIVING HISTORY VILLAGE, PHOENIX

Whiskey Is Road to Ruin
—Saloon motto

The Pioneer Restaurant, operated separately from the Pioneer Living History Village, is open seven days a week.

ACCORDING TO LEGEND, Whiskey Is Road to Ruin was the name of a saloon in Gila Bend, Arizona, during the late 1800s. These were the days of the Butterfield Stage, and the saloon served as a watering hole for passengers and anyone else who happened by. The Pioneer Restaurant at the Pioneer Living History Village, about 10 miles north of Phoenix, has been reconstructed from the original site.

On entering the restaurant, visitors step straight into history. A Brunswick-Balke-Collender bar greets everyone at the door. According to documents, this cherry bar is one of only two still in use from Arizona's territorial days (1863–1912). The other's location remains a mystery.

Manufactured in Iowa, the bar was freighted to New York, then shipped around Cape Horn to San Francisco, from which it was carted by a twenty-mule-team wagon to Virginia City, Nevada. Records fail to show exactly where in this booming mining town it resided, but in 1888 it was sold to a saloonkeeper in Jerome, Arizona. It made the 700-mile trip from Virginia City to Jerome by another wagon team.

However, this bar was not home yet. Later that same year, 1888, Joseph Mayer purchased the cherry beauty, which included a chocolate marble base, glass doors, mirrors, a liquor cabinet, and a table. He again packed it onto wagons and hauled it to his newly established town of Mayer, Arizona, 60 miles north of Phoenix.

Communal rags, used to wipe suds off a mustache, hung under the bar counters.

Unlike many brass foot rails, this iron rail is from a narrow-gauge track from the Crown King area in the Bradshaw Mountains.

The bar made one last trip in 1963, when it was moved to Pioneer Village. The Living Museum was started that same year by a group of civic leaders who were alarmed at the mountains of territorial history being bulldozed. In 1962, according to museum literature, the Robert Lockett family donated a state land lease to the newly created Pioneer Arizona Foundation. Since that day historic buildings from all over the state have been brought to Pioneer Living History Village for preservation and public education. Formally opened on February 15, 1969, it continues to grow.

But one doesn't have to pay the nominal museum entry fee to enjoy the Mayer Bar and the Pioneer Restaurant. It operates separately and is open after the museum closes.

The twenty-five-foot bar is amazing. Analyze every inch of it. Start at the foot rails. Instead of the typical brass seen on most bars, this rail is from a narrow-gauge train track from the Crown King area in the Bradshaw Mountains. All of the pieces are original—the marble base, the glass doors, the mirrors. All of it.

As was the custom of the time, the front bar had towel clips hanging from the underside. This allowed patrons, all of whom were men, to wipe the suds from their mustaches. However, modern health concerns and the U.S. Health Department frowned on the practice, and the towel clips were removed in the early 1950s.

This standing bar (all bars were "standing," as more customers could be accommodated) sports the gapped-tooth "dentrifice" railing on top, with four pillars on the back bar.

Who has leaned against this bar? Wyatt Earp—the twenty-first-century Wyatt Earp, great-grandnephew of the *other* Wyatt. Today Wyatt (II) performs with the Arizona Gunfighters reenactment

ARIZONA 32

group and has been known to come in from time to time to wet his whistle. Miners, mine owners, businessmen, and more than likely a few "sporting girls" from Virginia City, Jerome, and Mayer have leaned against this wooden social center, telling stories—some true, some not.

History

Pioneer Village is Arizona's largest collection of historical buildings in a village setting. There are log cabins, a farmhouse, an opera house, a church, a livery stable, a blacksmith shop, a school, and various stores that supplied services to towns; $7 for adults, $5 for children.

Getting There

Pioneer Living History Village is located half a mile west of I-17 at exit 225. Approximately 15 miles north of Phoenix, it is an easy on-and-off the highway. Open most days; there is an entry fee, but access to the bar is free. 3901 West Pioneer Road; (623) 465–1052; www.pioneer-arizona.com.

oppsite page, top left: A woodworker's delight, this Brunswick-Balke-Collender bar sports all the fine detailing of the day.

opposite page, bottom left: This spandrel—the triangular area between the mirrors—is decorated with dentils, egg-and-dart beading, and applied carving curlicues.

Reconstructed from nineteenth-century buildings, this pressed tin ceiling sets off the mahogany carvings.

Acanthus leaf designs were popular in the Victorian West.

Honky-tonk music flows over the Palace patrons today, the same as it has done for over a hundred years. The oldest frontier bar in Arizona, it was home to Virgil Earp and Doc Holliday.

The Palace

PRESCOTT

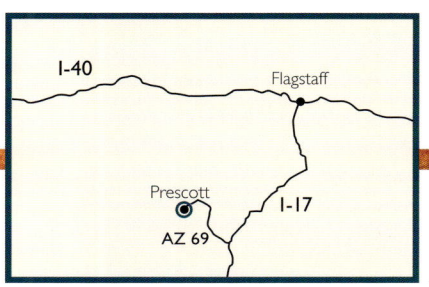

My only regret is that I didn't buy the Palace when I had the chance.
—Barry Goldwater

"FIRE! FIRE!" THE YEAR WAS 1900.

Those heart-stopping shrieks pierced the air like arrows. Flames marched down Whiskey Row, licked the wooden buildings, then, one by one, consumed them. Men scrambled. *Save the Palace.*

Unfortunately, the building itself could not be saved, but the wooden Brunswick-Balke-Collender bar sure could. Despite its weight and size, men lugged the mahogany masterpiece across the street and into the plaza. Not far behind came the back bar and the ice box.

Before fire took everything along this Arizona Territory town's business area, a few intrepid individuals gathered up as many whiskey bottles as they could carry and set up shop in the plaza. After the fire was out, the thirsty fire fighters toasted the ashes. A tent was soon erected in the plaza, and business continued as usual. The owner vowed to rebuild.

And rebuild he did. By 1901 the Palace Hotel and Bar, complete with barbershop and Chinese restaurant, was back in business. When it opened in 1877, before the fire, the Palace was more than just a place to slake a man's thirst. It became a labor hall,

The Palace was *the* place on Whiskey Row. Not only was it a watering hole, but it also served as the gathering spot for job information and elections.

where men came in to check on work available, as well as to discuss local politics. "It was the center of communication," says the manager, Katie Clayton. "The first telegraph machine was centered in the bar."

The standing bar itself has supported more elbows than almost any other in the territory. This piece of mahogany runs approximately thirty feet long and sits on a chocolate marble base. A brass foot rail anchors it. Believed to have been transported from New Jersey probably on a rail train, the bar took three months to get to Prescott and then was brought by mule train to the Palace.

Whose elbows have perched on this magnificent bar? Wyatt Earp, Doc Holliday, Big Nose Kate, who's buried there in Prescott, and Little Egypt, who belly danced her way into the hearts of patrons in 1910. Other elbows have belonged to rodeo stars such as Ty Murray and Trevor Brazile; the movie stars Hopalong Cassidy, John Wayne, and Steve McQueen; notables Senator Barry Goldwater, President Teddy Roosevelt, Willie Nelson, and Hank Williams Jr. Today Wyatt Earp can be seen regularly at the bar—and not as a ghost. Earp's great-grandnephew,

top left: Michael Breeden lugs a beer keg out of the 1880s ice box. This and the bar were carted across the street during the fire of 1900.

bottom left: This stamped tin ceiling is original to the 1901 construction.

above: Early day message board when the Palace was also a hotel and brothel.

ARIZONA 36

namesake of the famous lawman, performs at some Monday dinner shows.

Scenes from the movie *Junior Bonner*, starring Steve McQueen, were shot in this bar and restaurant.

The wooden floors of the Palace have darkened with age and the wear of boots. However, before it burned in 1900, the floor was inlaid with black marble tile. One interesting feature is on the north wall, an 1800s version of our "eye in the sky"—a small cubbyhole for an armed guard to sit in right above the safe. He carried a double barrel shotgun but only had to use it once. The safe dates from 1901. The tin ceiling in the dining room, also dating from 1901, sports the requisite bullet holes. Who put them there is still discussed.

As was common practice, the Palace was a hotel and brothel. Tunnels under the building are said to lead throughout Prescott and were used at one time to smuggle Chinese immigrants and opium. The Chinese helped build the railroad in Prescott, which was a major city in 1900. In its heyday Whiskey Row sported thirty-two bars in one block.

The Palace is always busy. According to its manager, Katie Clayton, about 75 percent of the customers are tourists, but they're treated like locals. "It's like a big family," she says. The Red Hat Ladies Club comes in, as does the male equivalent, the Red Shirt—Clampers Men, the first Monday of the month. Then there are holiday parties, wedding receptions, corporate events, even Irish wakes. Honky-tonk piano entertains on Sundays.

History

President Abraham Lincoln proclaimed Arizona a territory on February 24, 1863. Prescott, population 43,000, was named the territorial capital in 1864. In 1867 the capital was moved to Tucson, where it remained until 1877, when the politicians of Prescott got it back. It remained in

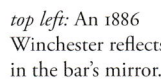

top left: An 1886 Winchester reflects in the bar's mirror.

top right: Details of this 1880s Brunswick-Balke-Collender bar attest to the craftsmanship of the day.

bottom: Oak batwing doors open into the saloon where honky-tonk music plays still today.

above left: Glass panels greet visitors as they step into the Palace.

above right: Dating from 1901, this safe was protected by the shotgun guard who sat perched directly above it. He only fired once.

left: Manager Katie Clayton tends bar. She was not here, of course, when the likes of Wyatt and Virgil Earp, Doc Holliday, and Big Nose Kate were patrons. The belly dancer Little Egypt performed here in 1910.

above: Applied carvings adorn the mahogany Brunswick bar.

ARIZONA 38

far left: Egg-and-dart trim runs across the top of the bar.

left: Handmade carvings wrap around the corner of the bar.

The city was named for William Hickling Prescott (1796–1859), who was considered one of the greatest American historians. The rise and fall of the Spanish empire kept him absorbed for over thirty years. His book, *The Conquest of Mexico* (1843), and other works were very popular before the Civil War.

Prescott until 1889, when Phoenix garnered enough clout to seize capital status.

Robert Groom surveyed the town site in 1864, using an old prospector's skillet for a transit. The first buildings were wooden structures, and Virgil Earp operated a lumber mill in Prescott before moving down to Tombstone with his brothers. Approximately seven hundred people called Prescott home then.

According to the *Roadside History of Arizona* (Mountain Press) by Marshall Trimble, "The first saloon, the Quartz Rock, was a rustic collection of timber with a plank for a bar. Tangleleg whiskey was dispensed by an army deserter who had lost his nose in an altercation." Originally perched on Granite Creek, the saloon later moved over to Montezuma Street, which soon became known as Whiskey Row.

One of the country's first rodeos was held in Prescott in 1888, the first paid-admittance event. Today it has grown into one of the largest and most prestigious, the Frontier Days Rodeo, held near the Fourth of July weekend.

Getting There

Prescott is 100 miles northeast of Phoenix. From Flagstaff, take I-17 south to U.S. Highway 169, get off at exit 278, then take U.S. Highway 69. From Phoenix, take I-17 north to Highway 69, get off at exit 262, and stay on Highway 69, which becomes Montezuma Street. Whiskey Row runs north and south on N. Montezuma Street between Gurley and Goodwin Streets, directly west of the county courthouse. The Palace, on the west side of the plaza, faces the courthouse. 120 South Montezuma; (928) 541–1996; www.historicpalace.com.

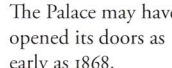

The Palace may have opened its doors as early as 1868.

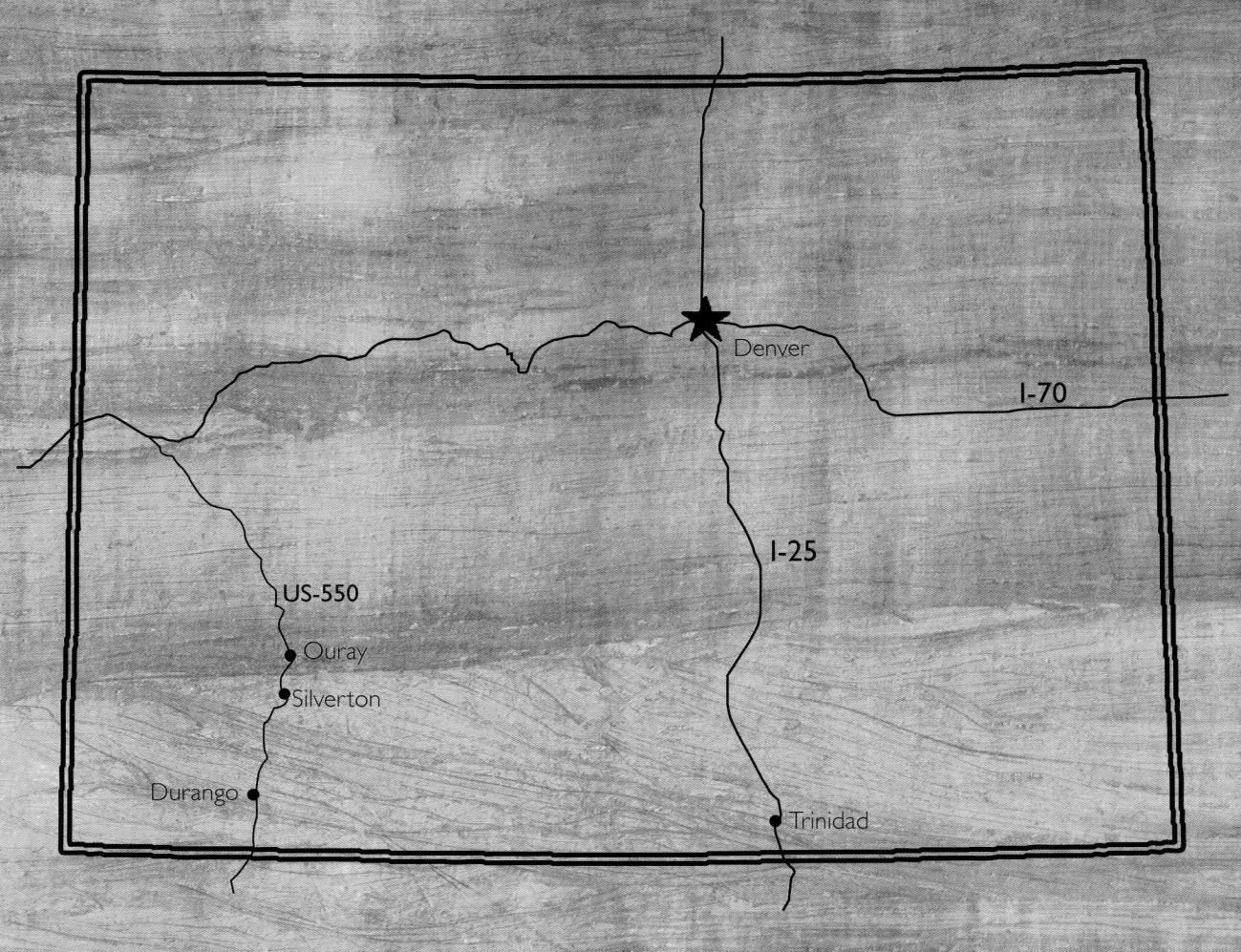

Colorado

Originally from Silverton, this bar was found in an old warehouse in 1957.

Diamond Belle Saloon

DURANGO

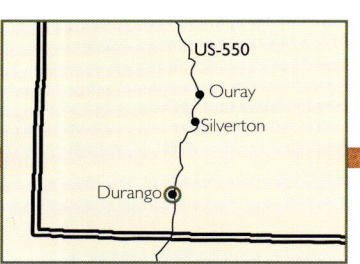

Work is the curse of the drinking class.
—Sign in the Diamond Belle

EARL BARKER JR., PART OWNER OF THE DIAMOND BELLE SALOON located inside the stately Strater Hotel, was poking around a dilapidated warehouse in Durango in 1957. His curiosity paid off. He discovered this ornate, cherry bar sitting in the back, waiting to be rediscovered and appreciated.

After much research, Earl Jr. discovered that this bar originally resided in Silverton, Colorado, no doubt brought across the Rockies by train from back East. The unusual finish of the back bar was achieved by painting it pink, then adding a second layer of paint mixed with stale beer so that it would "slip." The finish was "grained" by pulling a turkey or crow quill across the paint.

The history of the wooden front bar and back bar is obscure. Records of ownership are long lost, if they ever existed. Hard economic times, which ebbed and flowed, caused owners across the country to sell their bars. Prohibition sent many bars into hiding.

Henry H. Strater invested his Ohio family's fortune to build his hotel in 1887.

above: The back bar was finished with paint and stale beer.

below: Who caused this bullet hole is a matter of conjecture. Maybe Butch Cassidy and his gang?

They ended up in someone's shed under a tarp or were sent to Mexico for safekeeping. Some were converted into soda fountains. But before either of these fates, we know that the back bar saw wild times: the bullet hole in its drawer is testimony to this. Who put it there and why is a matter of conjecture and local lore.

Henry H. Strater realized his dream in 1887 when he opened this grand hotel and drugstore in downtown Durango. Soon the hotel gained a reputation as "the place to be." Social gatherings abounded, and the drugstore flourished. However, the silver panic of 1893 took its toll, and Strater lost his hotel.

Fast forward to 1954, when Earl Barker Sr. purchased all the stock of the Strater. Repairs and renovations made, Earl Sr. refused to change the corner office, which once housed the drugstore, into anything more than it already was: the Colorado Employment Agency. Earl Jr. waited for Dad to head to Phoenix for the winter in

Modern electricity lights this antique-style chandelier.

1957. Earl Jr. moved the agency out to create a new business, the Diamond Belle Saloon. He spruced up his newly discovered wooden bar and placed it against the east wall. On his return, Earl Sr. was pleased when he spotted several of his friends enjoying the new watering hole. He even approved of the sign painted on one of the Belle's walls: "Work is the curse of the drinking class."

Cowboys gather here every Tuesday to swap stories, poems, and songs. They no longer ride their horses and mules into the Belle, as they did just a few years back. The cowboys' antics have tamed down a bit over the years, but that one bullet hole in the drawer remains, spawning many theories in bar conversations.

What do astronaut Buzz Aldrin, director Steven Spielberg, and outlaw Butch Cassidy and his gang have in common? They have all stayed at the Strater Hotel in Durango. And the western writer Louis L'Amour occupied the rooms right above the saloon. It is said that the sound

 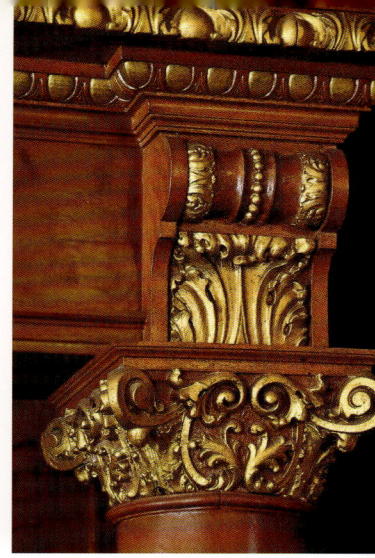

of glasses clinking, ragtime piano music, and patrons' laughter inspired his writing. Much of his Sackett series was penned here.

In addition to the above, record-holder balloonist Ben Abruzzo, actors Paul Newman and Robert Redford, locals—some famous, some not so famous—and visitors from the world over have leaned against this wooden survivor. Skiers, hunters, winter sports enthusiasts, summer campers, college students, and tourists who come in to ride the historic Durango & Silverton Narrow Gauge Railroad, whose station is right down the street, have lifted one in the Diamond Belle.

an average of $2.25 a day. The D&RG (now the Durango & Silverton Narrow Gauge Railroad hauls only tourists now (over 200,000 each year), but the railroad depot looks the same as when it was constructed in 1882.

History

Durango, from the Basque word *urango*, meaning "water town," was founded in 1880 when the Denver & Rio Grande Railway built a track to Silverton. Colorado Governor Alexander G. Hunt gave the town its name in honor of Durango, Mexico. The railroad established Durango as the hub of its rail system to transport ore from the mountains to Durango's smelter. Laborers who built the railroad were paid

Getting There

Durango, located in southwestern Colorado, is 107 miles south of Montrose, Colorado, and 212 miles north of Santa Fe, New Mexico. U.S. Highways 550 and 160 intersect in Durango. 699 Main Ave.; (970) 247–4431; www.strater.com.

top left: Egg-and-dart detailing, which was used by the Greeks in most of their designs.

top right: Acanthus leaf wood carvings decorate the top of the back bar.

right: The Strater Hotel became known as *the* place for social gatherings.

Sears, Roebuck and Co. sold bars, too. This one was brought to Silverton by rail in 1901.

Grumpy's Saloon

SILVERTON

The bullet holes are from the 1920s.
—George Foster, owner

WARNING! ONE STEP INTO THE GRAND IMPERIAL and you may become "swimmy headed." One look at the expansive, imposing bar—front and back—and you'll forget to breathe. The structure sits regally against one wall, holding court for its visitors.

Instead of a traditional Brunswick-Balke-Collender, as one would expect, according to owner George Foster, this bar is from Sears, Roebuck and Co. Ordered from a Sears catalog by the Grand Imperial's owner in 1901, it was shipped by rail to Silverton, where it was assembled. Original mirrors adorn the cherry and tiger maple back bar. *Impressive* is an understatement.

According to Foster, a sister bar, which was a relatively common occurrence, is located in the Old West town of Tombstone, Arizona. Where, exactly, is undetermined.

Whose elbows have been on this bar for the past 110 years? Silverton's undersheriff Bat Masterson for one. And we can be assured that lawman Masterson inspected each of the twenty-seven bars in town. It is said that it was Masterson who left a bullet hole in the famous ornate back bar. And while silver and gold flowed, Silverton boomed, bringing with it wealth and influential people.

The Grand Imperial Hotel, built in 1882, now houses Grumpy's Saloon.

Bat Masterson may have leaned against this Sears bar.

Victorian-era molding accentuates the ceiling and top of the back bar.

The Silverton *Democrat* reported on December 6, 1884, "There are 27 saloons in this mining camp, nine of them in the block opposite the hotel (Grand Imperial). . . . At night the uproar is hideous. . . . The betting and drinking are pretty heavy when the miners are freshly paid up; they revel in a beer at 14 cents a glass or two for a quarter, and get much foam and glass for the money."

The Grand Imperial Hotel, built in 1882, has watched Silverton expand and shrink, thrive and deteriorate, only to be reborn as a tourist and outdoor sports mecca. Built by Charles S. Thompson and Dr. S. H. Beckwith, the Grand Imperial was designed with business and government offices in mind. However, with so many saloons and only two hotels, the owners changed their minds and turned it into a hotel. Money flowed nonstop. The hotel served as a supply and social point for the more than ten thousand people (mostly men) living in and around the San Juan Mountains.

Locally made bricks and ironwork decorate the building's exterior. The narrow-gauge railroad brought in windows of French glass from Denver. In less than a year, this three-story, 22,500-square-foot hotel was completed and opened for business.

The Grand was located on the second and third floors, the ground floor left for retail space (two men's haberdasheries and two hardware stores). Brisk business soon encouraged the hotel to expand onto the ground floor, which accommodated a lobby and dining room.

When the lodging demand ebbed, the first floor became home successively to a barbershop, a bathhouse, a drugstore, a bank, a mining office, the Durango Meat Company, a soda fountain, a candy company, an Indian curio store, a post office, the Silverton *Standard* newspaper, a dining room and bar, the American Café, and then the Hub Saloon.

Today the Grand Imperial celebrates its rich heritage. The Victorian wallpaper provides an Old West backdrop for the Sears bar, in what is called affectionately Grumpy's Saloon. During the annual "Step Back in Time" celebration in June, the Grand hosts the informal Bordello Ball.

History

Mining—silver and gold. Silverton boomed when the precious metals were discovered in 1878. The Denver & Rio Grande Railway founded Durango in 1879, with the railhead arriving on August 5, 1881. Construction on the line to Silverton began in 1881 and was completed by July 1882.

Originally, the line was constructed to haul silver and gold ore from the San Juan Mountains, but passengers soon realized that what was truly precious was the breathtaking view. Tourists arrived in droves. In 1885 Silverton's population was 1,100, but with the opening of a toll road to the nearby mining town of Ouray, north of Silverton, and additional railroad track laid down in 1887, Silverton boomed.

But then came the Silver Panic of 1893 and the depression that accompanied it. Mines played out and shut down. People left. Winters were harsh. The thermometer has been known to plummet to minus 43 degrees with snow piled ten feet high in the street.

However, the "little train that could" kept right on chugging, bringing tourists and outdoor enthusiasts. The train that was designed to haul ore (it is estimated that over $300 million in precious metals have traveled over this route) now transports only visitors.

Those visitors step off the train onto Blair Street, which in its heyday was notorious for rowdy saloons and brothels. Bat Masterson, fresh from taming Dodge City, Kansas, was imported to subdue the criminal elements. From its beginning, Blair was infamous for its loud music and dance halls. Residents on the south end of that street were so mortified by its reputation that they petitioned the Silverton town council to have their end renamed Empire Street. Life has calmed down somewhat in recent years.

Getting There

Silverton is located between two rugged San Juan Mountain passes 50 miles north of Durango. From Durango, take U.S. Highway 550. 1219 Greene St.; (800) 341–3340 or (970) 387-5527; www.grandimperialhotel.com.

above: The Grand Imperial served as a supply and social point for more than ten thousand people in the 1890s.

This spandrel is decorated with egg-and-dart beading and applied carving curlicues.

The Brown Bear Café's owner, Patty Dailey, rests her elbows where Bat Masterson may have rested his. This custom-built bar dates to 1898.

Brown Bear Café

SILVERTON

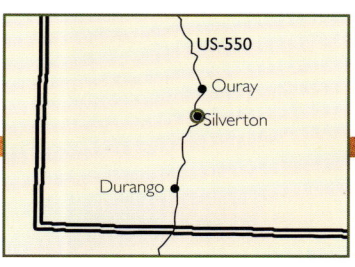

[It] used to be disco purple.
—Fred Dailey, saloon owner

IT IS HARD TO IMAGINE PLACING a magnificent wooden bar, both the front and back pieces, in storage in somebody's shed or garage and then forgetting about it. But that's exactly what happened to the beautiful oak bar now gracing the Brown Bear Café.

The current owners, Fred and Patty Dailey, say this bar was custom built in 1898 for the Silver Queen in Silverton. No one knows how long it sat there, quietly watching the antics of miners, politicians, businessmen, tourists, and railroad builders. Then at some point, possibly during Prohibition, it disappeared.

Fortunately, close to one hundred years later, in 1995, the front and back bars were discovered stored in that shed in Durango. Years of neglect were evident, including sixteen coats of "disco purple" paint, according to Fred Dailey.

The bar was returned to Silverton, and after a year of hard work—scrubbing, sanding, polishing—the beauty of this deeply grained oak bar sprang to life once more. From its first days in the Silver Queen and in the decades since,

Built originally as the Silverton Meat and Produce Company in 1893, the Brown Bear has housed various social and business groups since then.

Applied wood carvings run across the top of this custom-built bar.

Today it is hard to imagine that sixteen layers of purple paint once covered this handcrafted oak bar.

The Brown Bear's tin ceiling and antique mirrors add to the Old West ambience.

Bat Masterson, Silverton's under-sheriff, hundreds of miners, prospectors, railroad tycoons, railroad passengers, hunters, tourists, and locals have enjoyed this bar. And now you can, too.

The building, constructed in 1893, was originally the Silverton Meat and Produce Company. Various fraternal groups, including the Odd Fellows Lodge, the Forresters Lodge, and the Miners Union, held meetings upstairs. It was so popular that in 1919 the Woodmen of the World purchased the building. As would seem fitting, the ground floor returned to a saloon in 1933 when Prohibition ended. It was renamed the Pastime, then the San Juan Bar and Melodrama Theater.

And now it's the Brown Bear Café.

History

It's all about mining. In 1874 the Silverton district opened legally to miners. Over two thousand men poured in, from all across the United States, Europe, and China. By 1875 there were

Attention to detail sets off this beautiful oak bar.

sawmills, a blacksmith shop, a mercantile, a newspaper, a post office, smelters, and an assay office. Roads were opened and improved, but wagon travel was still treacherous over the mountains. Silverton is blanketed by an average of 200 inches of snow each winter. So when the Denver & Rio Grande Railway reached Silverton from Durango in 1882, it was greeted with great enthusiasm.

The mines boomed, drawing in silver and gold prospectors like magnets. By the turn of the century the area had a population of 5,000. Silverton was home to churches, fraternal lodges, women's clubs, a baseball team, a brass band, and even an ice skating rink. Dances were popular. And forty fully functioning saloons lined the notorious red-light district—Blair Street.

Like most mining towns, Silverton saw boom and bust years. Unfortunately, the final financial setback happened in 1978, when the Sunnyside Mine flooded. The mine closed in the early 1990s. Today the entire town of Silverton, population 500, is a National Historic Landmark. A favorite destination for train fans, historians, and outdoor sportsmen, Silverton retains its intrepid flavor.

Getting There

Silverton, nestled between Molas Pass and Red Mountain Pass in the San Juan Mountains, is located 50 miles north of Durango, Colorado. From Durango, take U.S. Highway 550.
1129 Greene Street; (970) 387–5630.

top: The cash register was invented by James Ritty, an Ohio saloonkeeper, in 1879. John H. Patterson bought the patent rights in 1884 and established the National Cash Register Company.

bottom: After Prohibition in 1933, the Pastime Saloon moved into what is now the Brown Bear Café.

Built in Iowa in 1886, this Brunswick-Balke-Collender bar has survived travel, isolation, and fire.

Silver Eagle Saloon

OURAY

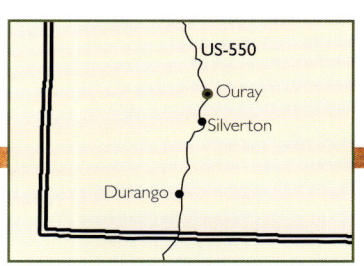

The building was built around the bar.
—Cheryl McDaniel, owner

THIS BRUNSWICK-BALKE-COLLENDER BAR has traveled more, seen more, and survived more than most humans do in a lifetime. Of course, the bar is over one hundred years old, so there's bound to be some wear on it. And all it takes to understand that long life is to step inside the Silver Eagle, where you know you've come face to face with history. And what a history it is.

Owner Cheryl McDaniel and her daughter Morgan explain the long journey this bar took to reach Ouray, the Switzerland of Colorado. "It was built by Brunswick in Iowa around 1886," says McDaniel. Destined for a Chicago hotel, this mahogany, cherry, and zebra wood beauty was designed as one of two identical bars, a practice that was quite common at that time. One would be placed on one side of the building where men could enjoy their brandy and fine cigars. The second, a replica of the men's saloon, housed the ladies, who enjoyed gossiping about the men on the other side. The bars sat literally back to back with only a wall dividing them.

There's no record of why they didn't grace that Chicago hotel. From 1886 to around 1900, one of them stood in Leadville, Colorado, fulfilling its purpose under men's elbows and listening to their tales. Then it was bought by a saloon

This facade was put in place around 1971, thus creating the Silver Eagle Saloon.

in Dallas, Colorado, an old railroad town, where it resided until around 1910. At that point it wended its way down to Ouray and was placed in a building down the street from where it now sits.

Enter local politics in the life of this bar. In the 1930s, 1940s, and 1950s, Ouray was rife with political and economic upheaval. Businesses were closing fast, and many vendors struggled just to keep their doors open. In 1951, however, the businessman who owned this bar saw a way out of his financial problems. After all, what good was insurance if you never used it? So he started a fire on the bar, hoping to burn down the entire building, collect the insurance, and go on his merry way.

He succeeded in burning part of the bar's top, but the fire was extinguished before the flames consumed more than the midsection. While he sat in jail, the assaulted and insulted wooden structure was moved to a warehouse behind the main street, where it sat collecting dust, dirt, and more than a few spider webs. In 1968 Jack and Vorsiel Scoggins, business owners in Ouray, bought it and chose what they envisioned as the perfect place for it. The problem was that there was no building, just an empty lot in the middle of the street where a building dating from the 1880s had once stood.

Once both side walls and the back wall were constructed, the Scogginses placed the bar along the north wall, then put in the front wall complete with door. The roof was added, and by 1971 the Silver Eagle Saloon was ready for business. Bruce and Cheryl McDaniel, the saloon's current owners, have polished and loved this survivor since 1986. While the burned center has been replaced, the entire bar has never been refinished. The mirrors are not original—the one on the far left was replaced in 1920—but the rest of this standing bar is original, including the copper and brass foot rails.

What happened to the sister bar? McDaniel has heard varying stories, but the most interesting comes from a "historic bar prospector." A few years ago this man stopped in at the Silver Eagle and was shocked to see its bar. He reported that he had seen its sister in Rico, Colorado. He said it had been in a Chinese opium den (which was legal at the time), and the resin from the opium had rotted the wood beyond repair, totally disintegrating it. True or not, it makes a great story.

Today not only do the tourists enjoy the McDaniels' company when seeking respite from a long day's summer shopping, or hitting the winter ski slopes, but the locals favor it as well.

The bar was placed against the north wall, and then the front wall and roof were added.

The Silver Eagle Saloon's owner, Cheryl McDaniel, and her daughter, Morgan, disclose bar details to the author.

History

Officially incorporated in 1876 and populated by four hundred determined miners, the town was named for the famous Ute chief, Ouray, who had signed a government treaty releasing the Ute's San Juan Mountains to settlers. By 1880 Ouray exploded with over 2,600 inhabitants. The town included a school, churches, a hospital, restaurants, saloons and brothels; hardware, clothing, and supply stores; and hotels and boardinghouses. In 1888 Ouray celebrated the arrival of the Denver & Rio Grande Railway. However, by 1893 the value of silver fell drastically, challenging the resolve of Ouray's residents. The town proved a survivor when Tom Walsh discovered one of the richest mines in Colorado—the Camp Bird gold mine, southwest of town. Walsh was known for compensating his miners well, and before he died he also gave Ouray a fully stocked library and saved the community hospital (now the Ouray Historical Museum) from financial ruin.

Getting There

Ouray is 40 miles south of Montrose on U.S. Highway 880, which becomes U.S. Highway 550, and 80 miles north of Durango on U.S. 550. The well-maintained single road into and out of Ouray is scenic but winding, with steep drop-offs at times. Winter driving can be challenging.
617 Main Street; (970) 325–4161.

This upstairs custom-made bar resided in Valdez, Colorado, before it moved to Trinidad in the 1890s.

This downstairs custom-made front and back bar comes from Valdez, Colorado, also.

Black Jack's Saloon

TRINIDAD

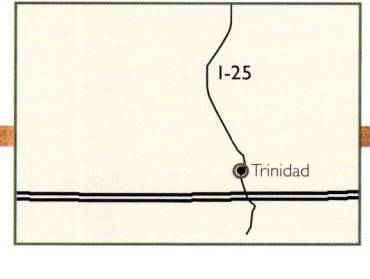

Where the spirit of the West lives on.
—Saloon motto

PRESSED TIN CEILINGS OVERHEAD AND hundred-year-old oak planking underfoot greet visitors as they step into Black Jack's Saloon. Shoes brush aside peanut shells, instead of the more traditional absorbent sawdust, strewn across the floor. Welcome to a slice of living Old West history. The homey ambience makes visitors feel at ease, just as it did when the likes of Black Jack Ketchum prowled the streets of Trinidad, maybe with his outlaw brother, Sam. This is where Bat Masterson, when he wasn't the town marshal, went looking for games of faro and cards, where Doc Holliday was held on bail, protected from trial by his friend Wyatt Earp.

Black Jack's Saloon started life as the Atlantic Bar around 1880. Later it became the Yellow Rose and was recently renamed Black Jack's. The building is in its original location, unlike the back and front bar in the upstairs saloon. The back bar is believed to have arrived at the Atlantic Bar around 1890 from Valdez, Colorado, several miles west of Trinidad. Known as a standing bar, it was designed for men to stand to drink, not sit. After all, owners could get more men bellied up to the bar if they stood.

Black Jack's sits on the old Santa Fe Trail.

left to right: Mule deer antlers create a stunning chandelier; Buffy, the white buffalo, roamed the plains of Colorado before coming to rest at Black Jack's; local animals hang around, watching the doings at Black Jack's.

Trophy heads of local, indigenous animals decorate the main dining/bar area. Black bear, elk, mule deer, and a pine martin "hang around" Black Jack's, observing the comings and goings of patrons. Buffy, the white buffalo, keeps an eye on the place. But nobody observes more closely than Spot, the longhorn steer, perched prominently in the center of the room. Spot is said to have been the last steer to cross the Pecos River during the last cattle drive. He probably wishes he had been first to cross.

Downstairs was a boxing ring and a livery stable. Writings and signage on the walls are still visible. The custom-made front and back bar is believed to be from a private house that served liquor in Valdez. One of the back bar's most impressive features is the delicate filigree work on the drawer pulls. Small flowers are carved into the pewter handles.

Also downstairs is the "hole in the wall," literally a hole, an intentionally unfinished portion demonstrating the building is made of slump rock. A picture of ol' Black Jack himself is painted in the middle of the rock. Today the downstairs is reserved for overflow events and special occasions.

Gracing the bar are brass foot rails and a mirror "that's getting old," according to Harmony Belle, the owner's daughter. If you listen carefully, voices of the past still linger within these walls.

According to legend, Wyatt Earp, Doc Holliday, Tom "Black Jack" and Sam Ketchum, and Bat Masterson rested their elbows on this bar, and possibly Trinidad's founder, Felipe Baca, whose house is now the Trinidad History Museum. While, as usual, there's no proof of their patronage, there is a strong possibility that they came in to hoist a few.

far left: While Butch Cassidy and his gang may have roamed through here, the hole in this wall shows slump rock, of which this building was made.

left: Many antiques add an Old West feel to this 1880s building.

below top: This drawer pull is unusual with its classic Greek debossed designs.

below bottom: Eighty-four companies sold cash registers between 1888 and 1895; only three, including National, survived.

More of a meeting hall today, Black Jack's is frequented by business development groups, the chamber of commerce, and Santa Fe Trail historians. Almost like the old days.

The Mountain Branch of the Santa Fe Trail (forged in 1822 by William Becknell) came right down Main Street, bringing with it hungry and thirsty men, women, and children. The men found refreshments at sixty-four establishments along Main or at many of the other bars found in basements and alleys elsewhere in town.

Today only a handful of saloons are left, mostly along Main. But thanks to preservation and careful management, they are making a comeback, at least in terms of making them family friendly.

Despite recent preservation efforts, many vestiges of the Old West are gone. Communal mustache rags, which hung under the front bar and were used to wipe foam from upper lips, were taken down by order of the U.S. health boards in the 1950s. More than likely, mustache rags won't be making a comeback. And gone as well are the spittoons that sat on the floor by the sturdy brass foot rails. For fear of spreading disease,

top: Details in the molding reveal feathers and flowers, dentils, and egg-and-dart designs.

bottom: Downstairs, the back bar mirror is surrounded with hand-carved wood appliqués.

The double Doric columns and the electric light are of an unusual design.

the spittoons were taken out during the influenza epidemic of 1918. Fortunately, gone also are the men-only rules of yesteryear.

History

Founded in 1842 by Mexican traders anxious to partake of the Santa Fe Trail opportunities, Trinidad and the surrounding area were still part of Mexico. However, in 1848 the Treaty of Guadalupe Hidalgo brought southern Colorado into the United States.

Led by Felipe and Dolores Baca, twelve families from Mora, New Mexico, settled in Trinidad in 1860. The fertile Purgatoire Valley held the promise of a rich life, and settlement was quick. The Bacas became prominent farmers, ranchers, merchants, and civic leaders. In addition to those of upstanding character, plenty of seedy characters were attracted by the chronic lawlessness of a frontier town. A handful of raids by the Ute Indians necessitated intervention by the U.S. Army. With adobe buildings, log dugouts, and slump rock structures lining Main and Commercial

Streets, Trinidad became a major center of commerce and agriculture for southern Colorado.

Officially incorporated in 1876, just prior to Colorado's statehood, Trinidad had already evolved from a small adobe village into a booming town. That year, about fifteen thousand tons of freight passed over Dick Wooten's toll road from Trinidad across the Rocky Mountains, through Raton Pass, and into Raton, New Mexico. In 1878 the Atchison, Topeka and Santa Fe Railway arrived in town.

Trinidad has grown from 560 citizens in 1862 to 2,226 in 1870 to 9,078 in 2000.

Getting There

Trinidad is 15 miles north of the New Mexico–Colorado state line and 200 miles south of Denver. From I-25, take exit 13B onto Main Street/U.S. Highway 160. 225 West Main Street; (719) 846–9501; www.blackjackssaloon.com.

Black Jack's started life first as the Atlantic Bar, then the Yellow Rose.

This Brunswick-Balke-Collender bar came from Ludlow, Colorado.

Monte Cristo Saloon

TRINIDAD

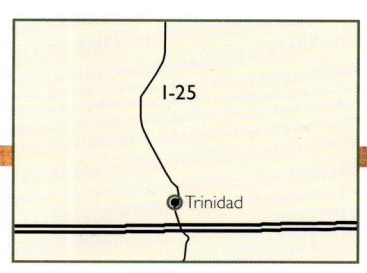

The bar is from a tent saloon.
—Mike Ryman, owner

BACK IN THE DAYS when the Old West was new, a saloon's role was vital, serving as communications central. Men gathered there to hear the latest on jobs, ranching techniques, labor disputes, news from the East . . . any information at all. And many of these saloons started life as tents.

It should not be surprising, then, to find that a magnificent piece of furniture, such as the one now holding court at the Monte Cristo Saloon, came from just such a tent saloon in Ludlow, Colorado. Before the bar sat in Ludlow, pieces of it migrated from Italy to New York in 1906, where it was assembled by the Brunswick Company. From there, it was shipped by train to Ludlow, where it graced the inside of a tent until 1913 or 1914, when it was freighted south to Trinidad. It was bought by the owner of the Monte Cristo and placed against the west wall and has served the community well since then.

The back bar is made of a relatively exotic wood, tiger cherry. The front bar, complete with brass foot rails, is made of cherry as well.

Built in 1910, this bar was one of sixty-four saloons along Main Street.

It is rumored that Bat Masterson put a bullet hole in the building that houses the Monte Cristo Saloon.

top left: Note the egg-and-dart molding and the torch with garland appliqué in this spandrel.

left: The egg-and-dart trim, a Greek pattern popular in Victorian design, signified birth and death.

top right: Carved column supports for the bar reveal wood aging well.

The back bar sports four columns, each adorned with a carving of a torch intertwined with curlicues. Over the three arches are now electric lights, replacing gas, the initial fixtures. Original leaded glass mirrors hang on either side of the big center mirror, which has been replaced. A close look at the right side of the back bar and mirror reveals a crack and hole that, according to the former owner, Loretta Day, "was caused by a bullet. Bat Masterson did that." The trim along the top of the back bar is a traditional Greek egg-and-dart pattern, popular with late-nineteenth-century bar makers.

Monte Cristo's gold-painted, stamped tin ceiling gives an aura of richness to this 1910 building. The barroom itself was once divided, with a wall running across the middle. One side was for men; the other, with a separate side entrance, for women. But as society matured, the wall has been removed and the side door bricked in. Whose elbows have rested here? It's hard to tell, but chances are that Bat Masterson's did, as well as miners, railroad workers, politicians, tourists, and locals.

This beautiful bar experienced an ugly beginning in Ludlow. This is the site of the infamous Ludlow Massacre, in which most of the tent city was wiped out in a coal mining dispute between labor and management. On April 20, 1914, Colorado National Guardsmen opened fire on twelve hundred striking coal miners and their families, including two women and eleven children. In total, twenty people died.

History

Incorporated officially in 1876, Trinidad grew from a tiny ranching community perched on the Santa Fe Trail. The famous first commercial highway runs right through town, down Main Street. Chronic lawlessness only served to add "character" to Trinidad. Characters such as Wyatt and Virgil Earp, Doc Holliday, Tom "Black Jack" Ketchum and his brother Sam, plus many other notables called Trinidad home.

In addition to mining, railroading has brought in thousands of people and jobs. Today, ranching, tourism, medical research, and Trinidad Junior College have stretched Trinidad's population to 9,100.

Getting There

Trinidad is 15 miles north of the New Mexico–Colorado state line and 200 miles south of Denver. From I-25, take exit 13B onto Main Street/U.S. Highway 160. 124 Santa Fe Trail; (719) 846–6314.

top: This is a creative use for a wagon wheel. Perhaps this one traveled the Santa Fe Trail.

middle: Since the Monte Cristo's owner is a motorcycle enthusiast, it's only fitting to have a wooden motorcycle inside.

right: The Monte Cristo Saloon's owner, Mike Ryman, chats with some of his regulars on a late afternoon.

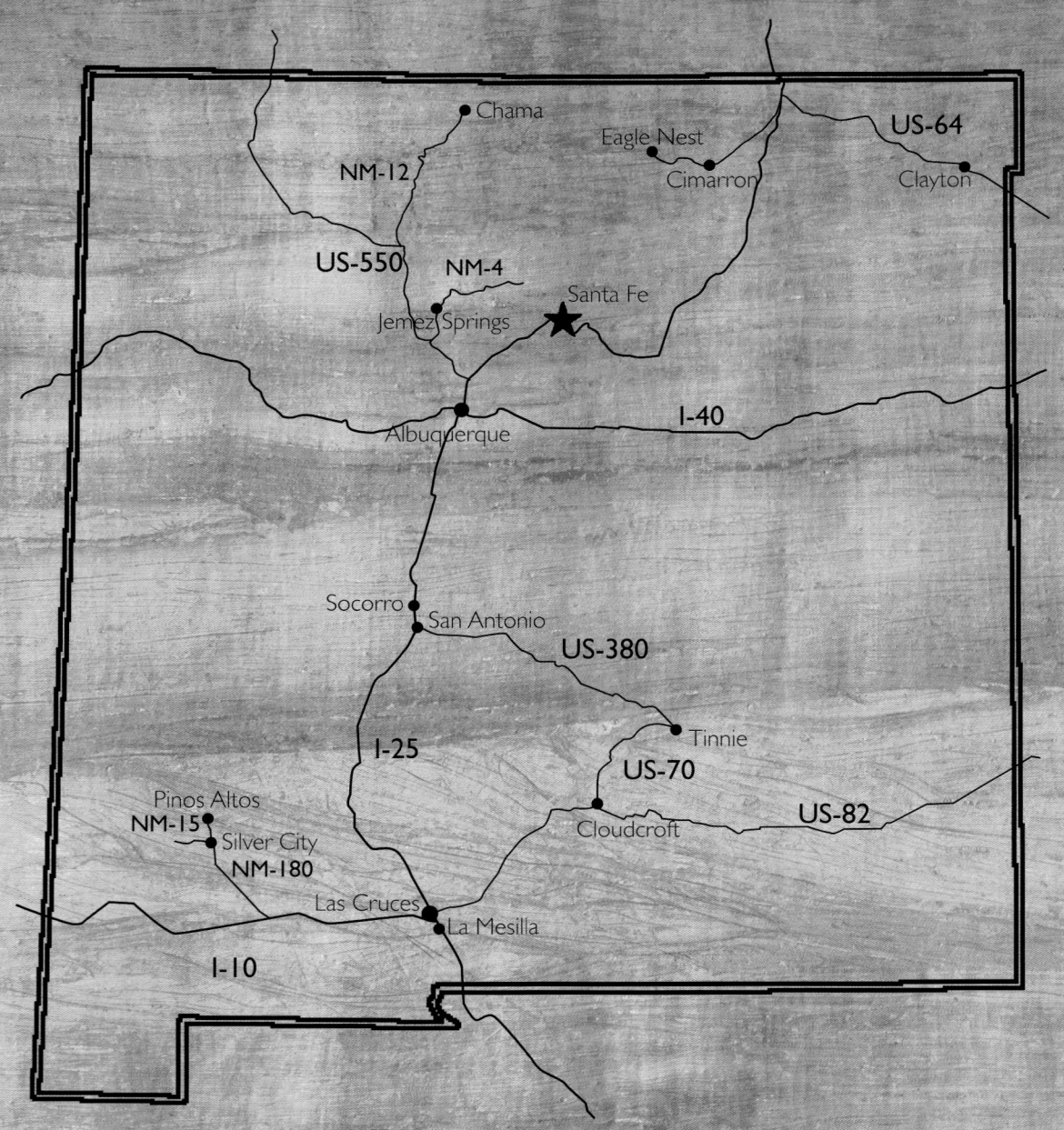

New Mexico

Won in a poker game, this oak bar traveled across New Mexico and came home to the Eklund Hotel in 1894.

Eklund Hotel

CLAYTON

The best drink in the house is water.
—Eklund's first bartender, 1894

THE HIGH-STAKES POKER GAME PLAYED ON IN THE SALOON until the rooster crowed. It all came down to the last hand. Carl Eklund, a Swedish immigrant and store and boardinghouse owner, had to put up all he had—$10—and that he had borrowed just to stay in the game. His saloon-owning opponent had only his cherry wood bar to put up. Their eyes met, heads nodded.

"Call," said Eklund.

The player from Capulin, New Mexico, splayed his cards. "Read 'em and weep. Full house." He reached for the pot.

"Not so fast, friend," said Eklund. He threw down his cards. "Four of a kind. Your bar's now mine."

The date was 1894. Eklund disassembled the front and back bars, packed the pieces onto mule-drawn wagons, and carted them 60 miles across the Kiowa grassland prairie to their new home in Clayton. After unpacking and setting up the cherry and oak bar, Eklund discovered that he had not only won the bar but also won the bartender. The luck of the draw bought bar and man.

But it was discovered within hours that the bartender was a teetotaler. He was reported to declare, "The best drink in the house is water." And he meant it.

Carl Eklund operated a store and boardinghouse until 1894, when he won the bar. Then he turned part of the store into a saloon.

On winning the beautiful twenty-foot bar, Eklund decided to open a saloon in part of his store. That wooden traveler now had a new owner in a new home in a new building.

The current bartender, Linda Trujillo, points out, "Our 'belly up' bar has never had stools in front of it." While the Eklund Hotel owners call it a "belly up" bar, others call such architecture a standing bar. Terminology aside, it was designed for men to stand while drinking. The idea was based on simple economics: more men would fit shoulder to shoulder than stool to stool.

Cowboys, drink in hand, lean back against the top plank and survey the rest of the saloon or chat with the men at their shoulders. But not having a place to sit has caused only one real problem at this Old West bar—and that is, according to a former owner, that over the century cowboys' spurs have raked into the wood. A close look near the bottom, just above the brass foot rails, reveals deep scratches and scars. Could some of those have come from Black Jack Ketchum, famous train robber? Or from cowboys coming off late-nineteenth-century cattle drives? Maybe from tough men trying to eke out a living on this dry prairie.

A landmark for travelers in the Southwest since the 1890s, the Eklund Hotel, a registered cultural property, began as a two-story rock building in 1892, the ground floor a store until 1894 when Carl Eklund brought in his elaborately carved bar. Unfortunately, exactly who made it has been lost to time. A close look at the back bar reveals the mirror is at least one hundred years old, and the mirrors on either side are beveled. Above the mirrors is Greek egg-and-dart molding, symbolizing the cycle of birth and death.

Photos of Clayton back in Black Jack Ketchum days adorn the walls. Maps of the Goodnight-Loving Trail remind visitors that not much has changed here in the past hundred years. There are still plenty of cows and cowboys around. A buffalo trophy, along with pronghorn antelope and deer, watch over the bar and restaurant patrons. The stamped tin ceiling, painted white, reveals two bullet holes—one from a celebrating cowboy who had

just won election as sheriff (but never served, as he soon went off to war) and the other hole from . . . well, no one is sure. One slug was recovered in the room upstairs, when it was remodeled, but the other bullet was never found.

To say that the Eklund Hotel is the center of the community would be an understatement. The chamber of commerce, the Rotary Club, and the Red Hat Society all meet here. Then there are skiers in winter, hunters in fall and spring, tourists in summer—locals and tourists alike come in to sit and swap stories. And, says one of the former owners, "lots of people come in to take photos."

Whose elbows have rested on this bar in the past one hundred years or so? More than likely outlaw train robber Thomas "Black Jack" Ketchum and his brother, Sam, and recently the singers Hal Ketchum (no relation to outlaws Tom and Sam), Randy Travis, and John Michael Montgomery, eleven times barrel racing world champion Charmayne James, and many politicos.

History

Clayton, named for Clayton Dorsey, son of U.S. Senator Stephen W. Dorsey, one of the area's developers and politicos, has long been a major stop on the trails of the West. Spanish explorer Francisco Coronado passed through in 1540 on his way to Kansas. In the 1860s large cattle drives on the Goodnight-Loving Trail used the Clayton area as a stopover and resting place. In addition, a portion of the Santa Fe Trail, the Cimarron Cutoff, ran just a few miles north of Clayton. In the 1880s freight lines from the railroad in Kansas passed through. Then another railroad, the Colorado & Southern, came to Clayton.

The arrival of the railroad in 1887 signaled the true beginning of Clayton, which was established that same year. Today Clayton, population 2,100 (according to the 2007 census), is a livestock shipping center.

Getting There

Clayton is 82 miles southeast of Raton, New Mexico, and 11 miles west of the Oklahoma and Texas state lines. U.S. Highway 64 intersects with U.S. Highways 87 and 412 in Clayton. 15 Main Street; (575) 374–2551; www.theeklund.com.

opposite, counterclockwise from left: Ornate drawer pulls adorn the back bar; called tiger striped because of the markings, this oak is favored by craftsmen for its exotic look; these mirrors are at least one hundred years old; the dentils and egg-and-dart molding run the length of the bar.

top left: Built in 1892, the Eklund was added on to in 1898 and 1905.

top right: Applied wood carvings set off the back bar arches.

right: Cowboys off the Goodnight-Loving Trail more than likely knocked back a few at the Eklund.

Bartenders Frank Pierce and Doug Strong pour a cold one for the locals and tourists who come through.

Laguna Vista Lodge
EAGLE NEST

2005 Best of the West Saloon
—True West Magazine

MINERS, FUR TRAPPERS, HUNTERS, cowboys, ranchers, outlaws, Easterners, madams—everyone frequented the Gold Pan Saloon, across from the El Monte Hotel. Drinks flowed, stories flew, and times were good. All activities centered around the custom-made bars, both front and back, which had started life in Chicago. Bought by the Gold Pan owner in 1890, the wooden structures were railed to Denver and then freighted by horse-drawn wagons to the high mountains of Eagle Nest. The twenty-five-foot oak bar was constructed in a curve, very unusual for that day.

Laguna Vista Lodge, originally the El Monte Hotel, was built with railroad ties.

This ceiling is lower than most. Bert Clemens, owner of the Laguna Vista, says that helps keep people from riding their horses into the saloon.

Like many saloons of the Old West, the Gold Pan caught fire and burned down. Despite the flames and personal risk, the patrons of that saloon, as well as the town's citizens, carted the front bar and the roulette wheel outside before the building was completely engulfed. Unfortunately, and to everyone's chagrin, the back bar perished.

The El Monte Hotel bought the surviving furniture and brought it across the street, where it still resides today. The saloon, locally known as the "Guney," dates to 1898, when gold nuggets from the mining camps in Baldy Town and Elizabethtown reigned supreme as legal tender.

The El Monte, which changed its name in the 1940s to the Laguna Vista Lodge, was built with "borrowed" or "liberated" railroad ties. The story goes that one winter the railroad was building a tunnel several miles away and decided to wait for the warmer summer months to finish. They left the ties unguarded. Apparently quite a few buildings in the Eagle Nest area have railroad ties in their framework.

The Laguna Vista Saloon sports a low ceiling—much lower than most buildings. Speculation as to why it is so low varies. Some say the lower ceiling makes it easier to heat (it's really cold in the winter, especially at this high altitude). Others say it's to keep people from dancing on the bar, and to keep the horses out.

But that didn't work. In fact, in the late 1970s a cowboy from a neighboring village rode a horse through the bar. The more unusual part to the story is that the cowboy wore boots, a hat, and nothing else but a smile—except for his strategically placed guitar.

The walls of the Laguna Vista Saloon are adorned with just the sort of trappings one would expect of a lodge in an old mining area: a horse headstall, an old saw, a wagon wheel, chaps, ropes, a deer head, a powder horn, and very old, very heavy ice or log tongs. A potbelly stove sits to one side, and a powerful heater warms cold hands and feet. The narrow oak planks sing and squawk with every step across the floor. And it's because of that very cacophony that one of the bartenders knows the place has a ghost. One night, he reports, when he was alone, ready to close up, the floor creaked step by step across the room. He said it's a female ghost waiting for her new husband.

Besides the ghost, who else has floated past that 1890s bar? Governors, politicians, the cast and crew of *Lonesome Dove*, international tourists, locals, cowboys, ranchers, Robert Duvall, Dennis Weaver, Lucille Ball, and several astronauts. In fact, says owner Bert Clemens, "Every candidate running for governor who won has held a rally here."

Clemens is in the process of renovating the entire lodge. Next to the saloon is the former whorehouse, complete with original wallpaper and a couple of dresses. He plans to open it as a high-end restaurant and venue for weddings and private parties.

It is easy to see why the Laguna Vista was voted "Best of the West Saloon" in 2005 by *True West Magazine*.

Bartenders like Doug and Frank help make the West and the saloon a great place to lift a couple of glasses.

History

Utes and Jicarilla Apaches roamed the area in search of game and eagles' feathers for ceremonial functions. Ranchers and farmers shared the land with the Indians in the 1870s. In 1873 Charles and Frank Springer founded the CS Ranch on the Cimarron River. The brothers built a dam in 1916 designed to store the surplus waters of the Cimarron River for power plants, mining, and irrigation. It is said that eagles built nests on the sides of the dam, giving the village its name.

Eagle Nest Lake lured fishermen as well as entrepreneurs, who built businesses and transformed the quiet farming community into a tourist mecca, providing entertainment for the visiting cowboys, fishermen, and tourists. In addition to timber, one of the biggest industries was cutting and selling ice from the lake. T. D. Neal hired men to drive out on the lake and cut block ice, which was then stored in icehouses filled with sawdust. Jobs were scarce in the 1920s, and many families survived the winters by ice cutting and animal trapping.

Also in the 1920s illegal gambling was introduced to the area. Eagle Nest became a popular spot for politicians and travelers along the road from Santa Fe to the horse racetrack in Raton. Visiting dignitaries were said to have caused quite a ruckus with their gambling, drinking, and carousing.

Quieter now, Eagle Nest is filled with arts and crafts shops, lodging, restaurants, and, of course, saloons. This mountain town has seen the addition of new sidewalks, streetlights, park benches, and flowerboxes. Main Street, less than a mile long, features numerous stores carrying locally made goods. In 2000 the population of Eagle Nest was 306.

Getting There

Eagle Nest is about 50 miles south of the Colorado border and 130 miles west of the Texas/Oklahoma border. It is 160 miles northeast of Albuquerque, 32 miles east of Taos, and 64 miles southwest of Raton. From I-25, take exit 419 west onto U.S. Highway 64, 43 miles. (800) 821–2093 or (575) 377–6522; lagunavistalodge.com.

opposite, top: Log tongs or ice tongs? Both were used in this part of New Mexico.

opposite, bottom: Eagle Nest is often the coldest town in the state. This stove warms even the coldest hands on snowy days.

right: Separating the customers from the barkeeps, this brass rail is not only ornamental but also functional.

This cherry bar survived a 1925 fire, thanks to firemen who stood on the roof and sprayed water all around.

Foster's Hotel
CHAMA

The bar is from Chicago, then Italy . . . or France.
—Rebecca Nuño

FOSTER'S HOTEL RADIATES ENOUGH HISTORIC CHARM to fill a book. Pictures painted by famous people adorn the walls. Wooden floors squeak and moan under footfalls. And the old cherry bar holds court over the entire lower floor of the building.

Rebecca Nuño, the owner's daughter, points out that the bar was originally from Chicago. But it was made in either Italy or France. Who made it and exactly when have been lost over the past more than one hundred years. Nevertheless, its size, color, and detail work are darn impressive.

The front bar runs a healthy twenty feet, enough room for patrons to comfortably belly up. The sixteen-foot back bar, also of cherry, houses the original ice box, set in the middle. Lined with tin and well insulated, the ice box kept the beer well chilled.

The mirror on top of the back bar is not antique. In fact, it is only about seven years old. It seems that a few years ago, a patron, angry at another, picked up a stool and—just like in old Westerns—hurled it. The intended target ducked and . . . well, you know what

Foster's is the oldest surviving commercial building in Chama.

top: The iron foot rail was part of an old train track.

bottom: The brass latch on the ice box still works well.

happened. A former bartender who witnessed the unfortunate wreck says, "It's too bad that happened, but now we only have pieces of that ol' mirror." The chair missed all the bottles but hit the mirror squarely in the middle. It was seven years ago—the bad luck should run out any day now.

At the base of this cherry bar, a portion of an iron train track serves as the foot rail, brought from the Cumbres and Toltec Narrow Gauge Railroad yard, one block south of Foster's. Train passengers alight from their half-day excursion and fan out up and down the main street of Chama, with Foster's usually in their sights. A restaurant adjoins through a set of swinging doors but is separate from the bar area.

So who frequents this rustic establishment? Who puts their elbows where Italians or Frenchmen or Chicagoans did? The list is long. Foster's is an official stop for motorcycle runs. Locals stop in often, and celebrities such as Beau Rivers, Willie Nelson, Mel Gibson, Johnny Cash, Kevin Costner, and the cast and crews from the movies *Indiana Jones* and *Cinderellas of Santa Fe* have hoisted a few. Many governors and "lots of dignitaries" have elbowed up at that bar. Maybe even the famous Old West gunman Clay Allison.

When it was young, Chama was a rough and tough town, a place where the law looked the other way. Built in 1881, Foster's is the oldest surviving commercial building in Chama. In its original incarnation, Foster's was a saloon, dance hall, and brothel. Another wing was added during the 1920s, which meant closing down the second story. Although no longer in service, those upper rooms are still dressed in their original wallpaper.

Due to a devastating fire in 1925, most of the original buildings in Chama are gone. What saved Foster's were the fire fighters who used its roof as command central, spraying water completely around the hotel. In the end, nothing, not one board, was even singed.

Listed on the National Historic Register and the State of New Mexico Historical Register, Foster's maintains a rustic feeling. But there's another interesting aspect of this building. Many people, locals mostly, claim that a ghost roams the area. They say an old man with a beard, wearing dirty jeans and a blue shirt, stands in the doorway to the restaurant and watches bar patrons. Maybe he's just hoping somebody will offer to buy him a beer.

In 1925, when the town burned, so did the Harvey House restaurant and hotel. Harvey Houses sprang up all along the railroad route heading West, providing fine dining for train passengers. Foster's became the new Harvey House, and railroad workers were given yellow coupons good for showers or a room. One can only imagine they also had a libation while there. And rested their elbows on the bar.

History

The Chama area is home to the Jicarilla Apache Nation, whose permanent reservation was established in 1887. Today gas and oil production have helped make the Jicarilla a wealthy and progressive nation. In 1598 don Juan de Oñate

left: This tiger cherry column is capped with a decorated abacus, the topmost member of the capital.

right: Carved wood appliqué sets off the end of the front bar.

Getting There

Follow U.S. Highway 285/84 north from Santa Fe, then U.S. Highway 84 north to Chama. Foster's is on the main road, at 4th and Terrace Streets, near the train depot. (505) 756–2296; wwwfosters1881.com.

founded the first European settlement in the West near the confluence of the Rio Chama and Rio Grande.

Consisting mainly of tents, just like other towns starting out in the late 1870s, Chama, 12 miles south of the Colorado border, was very prosperous. Entertainment was found in saloons and gambling houses. Moonshine warmed bellies on cold winter nights. Chama grew into a lawless town almost overnight. Outlaws such as Clay Allison and his gang often held up the railroad pay car.

But it took the railroad to make the biggest impact. In 1880 the Denver & Rio Grande began construction of the San Juan extension, passing through Chama. Freight and passenger services took off in 1881, bringing jobs, tourists, cattle, and lots of money. Now tourists are the only commodity carried by the rails. Most locals work for the railroad, in the tourism industry, and for timber and mining businesses.

top: The Cumbres and Toltec Scenic Railroad is across the street from Foster's, so the train motif is emphasized in the bar.

right: Chama receives several feet of snow each winter. The owner's car was the sad recipient of built-up snow that slid off the roof.

Originally housed in Raton, this bar traveled to Portales, Santa Fe, and now Cimarron.

Express St. James Hotel

CIMARRON

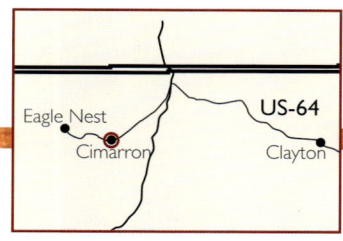

Where Legends Live On.
—Hotel website

"Jacks are wild," the cowboy muttered. He dealt the cards while a woman in red leaned over his shoulder.

"What's the ante?" asked a hotel visitor, awed at the authentic dress of the men hunched around a card table. He eyed the woman. Striking. Must be Old West reenactors come for the weekend, he thought.

"Two hundred dollars," another cowboy said.

"Too rich for my blood," the tourist admitted. He wished everyone a good game and went to his room on the second floor of the Express St. James Hotel. As he drifted off, he thought about rejoining the game, but the players' chatter had quieted.

The next morning he greeted the clerk at the front desk and inquired who had won the big game the previous night. Eyes wide, she then frowned. "What game? You were the only guest in our hotel last night." Thankful he was checking out, nevertheless the guest kicked himself for not sitting in on a hand.

The famous St. James Hotel has hundreds of ghost stories and is long famous not only for its ethereal permanent guests and but also for its riotous history. As I

Opening in 1872 as a saloon, the St. James Hotel grew a wild and woolly reputation, as well as an upper story, which turned it into a refined hotel.

left: Once gas, these lights are now electric.

below left: True craftsmanship was involved in constructing this bar. Notice the matched wood patterns.

stepped into the lobby, I was awed by its nineteenth-century glory. The reported ghosts, which appear in mirrors and hallways and, yes, even conduct poker games, are only one reason I chose to revisit this hotel.

Through the well-appointed lobby, its walls tastefully adorned with paintings, and around the corner is the bar. This was at the top of my list of reasons for coming, the historical ambience a close second. While this outstanding flagship bar spans the newly remodeled saloon, it is not original to the St. James. For sixty years, it resided only 40 miles northeast of Cimarron.

Originally housed in the Big Six Saloon in Raton, New Mexico, this mahogany masterpiece dates from around 1880. Like so many old bars, this one has done its share of traveling. It entertained thousands of miners in Raton and then, around 1940, moved to the Roosevelt Hotel in Portales, New Mexico, then relocated to the Hotel St. Francis in Santa Fe, New Mexico, in about 1970. It graced that hotel for almost forty years. In 2009 it was purchased by the St. James's new owner, Robert Funk, and returned to northern New Mexico.

The mirrors are old, more than likely original, too, as is the brass footrail. The lights, initially gas, are now electric.

The back bar, sporting four Ionic columns, is topped with traditional Greek egg-and-dart trim. A torch emblem spandrel, with intertwined leaves forming a wreath, decorates the front of this section. Not to be missed are the expertly matched wood grain patterns.

Whose elbows have been planted on this bar? Raton, known for its mining and ranching industries and as a Santa

top left: Carved wooden spandrels perch on either side of the original mirror, which is framed by egg-and-dart beading.

left: Brass foot rail supports are decorated with engravings.

Worn brass latches on the back bar's cabinet testify to the good times.

At least twenty holes "decorate" the ceiling. The St. James earned its reputation as "the place to be" on the Santa Fe Trail.

Fe Trail resting place, undoubtedly boasted hundreds, probably thousands, lifting a few. The likes of Wyatt Earp, Doc Holliday, and Bat Masterson rode through. Did they stop and hoist a brew? We'll never know for sure, but the chances are quite good that they did.

In Portales, more ranchers, farmers, railroad workers, tourists, and locals leaned against it, elbows earnestly at rest. And in Santa Fe it saw its share of movie stars and political celebrities for forty years. And now at the Express St. James, locals, tourists, and assorted celebrities all belly up to this fine bar.

History—St. James Hotel

Constructed during a time when law and order in Cimarron were nonexistent, the saloon quickly gained a reputation as a place of violence. It is said that twenty-six men were shot and killed within its adobe walls. Built in 1872 by a Frenchman, Henry Lambert, it was referred to familiarly by locals as "Lambert's Place."

Lambert built rooms above the saloon in 1880; the name changed from "Place" to "Inn" and eventually became the St. James Hotel (the exact reason and reference have been lost to time). In the construction of the new rooms, the existing roof became the new second story, so Lambert added several layers of wood on that floor to deflect stray bullets shot from down below. In 1901 Henry Lambert's sons, Fred and Gene, replaced the roof of Lambert's Inn and found more than four hundred bullet holes in the ceiling above the bar.

Closer inspection of the saloon's tin ceiling reveals at least twenty bullet holes. If you stand still, I swear you can hear honky-tonk music, shuffling cards, and the jangling of cowboys' spurs.

My own boots clomping up the stairs and down the hallway, I stop and admire the wooden tables, Victorian

This National cash register has held money from a wide range of patrons, from trail drovers to senators.

chairs, beds, a roulette table, window coverings, flocked wallpaper—all looking authentic. And they are—not only of that period, but most are original to this hotel.

Sited smartly on the Mountain Branch of the Santa Fe Trail, the St. James was considered one of the most elegant hotels west of the Mississippi. Around 1931 a new owner from Switzerland renamed it the Don Diego. When Ed Sitzberger bought the place in 1985, he reinstated the original name. Robert Funk bought it in 2009 and added "Express" to the moniker, making it the Express St. James Hotel.

This establishment has had its share of the famous and infamous. Wyatt Earp and his brother Morgan and their wives spent three nights at the St. James on their way to Tombstone, Arizona. Jesse James stayed here several times, always in Room 14, signing the registry with his alias, R. H. Howard. James's killer, Bob Ford, also lingered at the St. James.

Cimarron was a rest stop for herds of cattle being driven to markets and railheads.

NEW MEXICO 86

Buffalo Bill Cody, a goat ranch manager for the land baron Lucien Maxwell, met Annie Oakley at the hotel and began to plan and rehearse their Wild West Show. Other notables who have graced the historic inn include train robber Black Jack Ketchum, Union general Philip Sheridan, explorer Kit Carson, card shark Doc Holliday, outlaws Billy the Kid and Clay Allison (who allegedly danced naked on the bar—not *this* bar, the original one), lawmen Bat Masterson and Pat Garrett, artist Frederic Remington, territorial governor Lew Wallace, and writer Zane Grey.

History—Cimarron

Cimarron, Spanish for "wild" and "untamed," was established in the 1840s on the Mountain Branch of the Santa Fe Trail. The trail began in Independence, Missouri, stretched across the plains, and then divided near Ft. Dodge, Kansas, one route traversing the steep Raton Pass and the other taking a longer but tamer direction south.

With its seasonal river, Cimarron was a favorite watering spot for drovers pushing herds of cattle between Leavenworth, Kansas, and Santa Fe, New Mexico. This town was also a stage stop on the Santa Fe Trail and a welcome respite for weary travelers.

Once home of the Jicarilla Apaches and Utes, Cimarron became the hub of a mining and ranching empire when Lucien Maxwell, heir to the two-million-acre Beaubien-Miranda Land Grant (twice the size of Rhode Island), built his center of operations here after moving 12 miles north from Rayado.

When the railroad came through Raton, ending the need for the Santa Fe Trail, Cimarron's population dwindled. A 2007 census shows 832 residents. Once lawless, this charming and peaceful village today echoes the sights and sounds of its historic past. Ruts etched in the earth by the passing of emigrant wagons on the Santa Fe Trail are still evident. But history is not just evident here; it is revered.

Getting There

From I-25, 5 miles south of Raton, take U.S. Highway 64 west, exit 446. Cimarron is approximately 40 miles on a good, two-lane highway. Watch for antelope, deer, and cattle that tend to wander onto the road. The Worthington NRA Center is also on this road. 617 S. Collison Ave.; (888) 376–2664 or (575) 376–2664; www.exstjames.com.

In 1947 the handmade bar was cut in half when the owners added a restaurant and made a doorway.

Los Ojos Restaurant and Saloon

JEMEZ SPRINGS

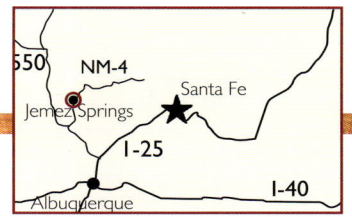

Thanks for making us famous.
—Brooks and Dunn, country singers

YOU KNOW YOU HAVE ARRIVED SOMEWHERE SPECIAL when you peek inside the Los Ojos Restaurant and Saloon. Granted, the bar itself, the wooden plank in the southern half of the building, while rustic and totally suited to this mountainous area, isn't truly *old* or very unusual. But what is unusual is everything else.

The building started life as a sheep dip barn around 1920. Jemez Springs backs onto the Jemez Reservation, and there are, still today, plenty of sheep in the area. The barn turned into a mercantile and then was used as a school until 1947, when it became a saloon owned by the Abousleman family. The red pine bar ran the entire length of the north wall, spanning about thirty feet. The tin ceiling, originally a cream color, has been darkened by fireplace smoke and time. It sports a few bullet holes courtesy of a local "character." Residents shake their heads and sigh when asked for a name, but they refuse to reveal which Jemez resident did the deed. Both the floor and the ceiling are original to the 1920s building, as are the windows.

Country music duo Brooks and Dunn liked Los Ojos (the Eyes) so much that they made their first music video here.

top: Made by a local resident, Joe Archie, more than forty years ago, these aspen and red pine stools were used in the movie *Hi-Lo Country*.

bottom: This bearskin has been hanging around since 1978, when it was donated by a man from Albuquerque. The ceiling was once cream but has darkened from age and soot.

While the bar itself may not stand out, the barstools certainly do. Hand-carved specifically for this bar by a local artisan, Joe Archie, well over forty years ago, these stools are made from aspen and red pine. And they're famous. The movie *Hi-Lo Country* rented them. Look closely, you may spot them in the movie.

Not to be missed are the antiques on the walls. The hides of bears shot by locals hang on the wood and adobe walls. Old saddles, photos, and rifles crowd around, creating a genuine Old West feel. Notice the hats over the door. These were worn by locals and loyal patrons who have since passed away. A fitting memorial.

Perhaps the most amazing animal adorning the wall over the bar is a Barbary sheep. Notice the front legs. Los Ojos owner, Pamela Grider, along with most of the customers, wonders where the back end went. She's looked on the other side of the wall more than once, as you probably will.

Throughout the last ninety years, the previous sheep dip barn has been expanded and now sports an interior restaurant and an outside patio. The menu lists Mexican food and hamburgers.

Who hangs out at Los Ojos? It seems that everyone does. Lots of locals, cowboys, hippies, bikers—anybody hungry or thirsty. And tourists, lots of tourists, especially in the summer. Actors Jeff and Beau Bridges have been here, as have Aiden Quinn and Dean Stockwell. According to Grider, the band Journey "loves it here" and stops in whenever they're nearby.

A fitting reminder of the men who passed through and on.

But Los Ojos' major claim to fame is as the site of the first Brooks and Dunn music videos. This famous country duo shot "Next Broken Heart" here and used the exterior in their second video.

And if internationally recognized musical groups coming and going aren't enough, Los Ojos is a sponsor of Toys for Tots, in conjunction with a motorcyclists' Christmas charity drive. It also houses the Scrabble Club, a senior citizens group, the Ski Club, and has hosted square dances. "We support charities and raffles," says Grider. "We give away a lot of dinners."

The waitstaff at Los Ojos is as intriguing as the clientele. One server is a former Olympic runner who came to Jemez Springs to train because of its high altitude. She liked the town and stayed.

Across the road from Los Ojos stands a line of cottonwoods, sentinels watching the doings of the bar. Judging by their size, they must be at least a hundred years old. What stories they could tell!

left to right: What happened to the back end of the Barbary sheep?; try riding this for eight seconds. Old West ambience at its finest: local deer that didn't get away.

History

Possibly since as early as 2500 BCE the area of Jemez Springs has been populated by native peoples, most recently the Towa tribe. It was the Spanish explorer Francisco Coronado and his men who first came through in the 1540s and began mapping the area. San José de Guisewa, one of the largest and most important mission churches in the area, was constructed by Native labor between 1620 and 1621. The church was destroyed in the 1680 Pueblo Revolt. It was not until the 1800s that farmers, sheepherders, and ranchers occupied the area.

Natural hot springs that have bubbled up for centuries beckon the weary, the frail, the infirm, and the tourists who simply want to soak in their warm mineral waters, which are said to have special healing powers. Jemez Springs was incorporated as a village in 1955, and along with that came telephone service. New Mexico State Highway 4 was first paved through the valley in 1949. A recent census shows 380 full-time residents, with about half again as many part-time residents.

Getting There

Jemez Springs is 60 miles northwest of Albuquerque. Take I-25 north to Bernalillo, turn west onto U.S. Highway 550, then north on U.S. Highway 4. (575) 829–3547; www.losojossaloon.com.

top right: The leaded-glass front door, made by the original owner's son, bids welcome to all hungry and thirsty visitors.

right: A well-worn deer antler makes a fine handle.

This oak bar has seen everyone from college students to atomic scientists.

Capitol Bar

SOCORRO

Everything centers here.
—Linda, bar manager

IT IS SAID THAT JUDGE ROY BEAN HELD COURT in the Capitol Bar. Whether he did or not doesn't really matter. What *does* matter is that this bar is a fun, happening place today. And it is the wooden bar that holds court.

In 1896 Socorro boasted the territory's largest population, reaching well over 3,000 residents. At that time more than thirty bars were built to satisfy thirsty miners, ranchers, gamblers, residents, and even outlaws. The Italian immigrant brothers Giovanni and Tobaschi Biavaschi built their saloon and served the finest wine anywhere. Giovanni, a winemaker from Valtellina, Italy, was said to be flamboyant and a bit of a con man. But he made delicious vino.

A few years down the road, the brothers sold the bar to Amos Green, a justice of the peace. Not only did he hold court here, but he jailed people in another part of the building. He also performed weddings here. It is said that he charged the groom based on the bride's beauty.

When Fred Emilio bought the Biavaschi bar, he changed the name to the Green Front (in honor of Judge Green) and then painted the front green.

Built by two Italian immigrant brothers, the Capitol Bar has anchored the east end of Socorro's plaza since 1896.

As a tribute to Nichele Nichols, Lt. Uhura of *Star Trek* fame, a starship hangs from the ceiling.

The "Cap," as it's affectionately known, is a hangout for college students, some whom no doubt instigated attaching an alligator to the ceiling.

During Prohibition the Green Front operated as a pool hall and speakeasy. For twenty-five cents, their moonshine was reputed to be the best in town. After Prohibition Emilio's bar became the first legalized bar in Socorro.

In 1937 Emilio's sons, Frankie and Willie, became owners and changed the name to the Capitol Bar and moved it next door. However, that building burned down in 1940, so the brothers moved back to where they had originally started. Now under the ownership of the DeBrine family, it is still called the Capitol Bar (known locally as "the Cap") and Socorro's oldest watering hole.

The oak bar, complete with brass foot railing, takes up most of one wall and has had thousands of elbows on it. Possibly a really rowdy elbow has been on this bar: local legend lawman and gunman Elfego Baca. Not quite as rowdy was actress Nichele Nichols of *Star Trek* fame. Before her, scientists who tested the atomic bomb at the Trinity Site, about 30 miles away, also sat here.

Other famous patrons were state dignitaries, local celebrities, various bands (some famous, some not), and lots of students, called "techies," from the local state college, New Mexico Institute of Mining and Technology.

History

First Socorro was. Then it wasn't. In 1598 Juan de Oñate led a group of Spanish settlers north from Mexico through the Jornada del Muerto, a deadly stretch of waterless desert south of present-day Socorro. As the group emerged from the desert, extending hundreds of miles into Mexico, Piro Indians of the Teypana Pueblo met them and provided water and food. To show their gratitude, the Spaniards renamed the pueblo "Socorro," meaning "help" or "aid."

But the Pueblo Revolt of 1680 wiped out the pueblo, its inhabitants, and settlers of the surrounding area, by now heavily populated by Spaniards. Not only did the Tewa and

Pueblo Indians kill and drive off the Spaniards, but they razed and burned everything. It was not until 1800 that the Spanish governor ordered Socorro rebuilt. However, that did not officially occur until 1815. Then, in 1850, New Mexico became a U.S. territory and Socorro had a population of 543, including the hundred soldiers stationed there.

According to Socorro's official website, the arrival of the railroad in the 1880s brought miners, merchants, and cattlemen to Socorro County. To the west, Magdalena became the center of mining activities and the "End of the Trail" for cattle drives from farther west. The town of Socorro boasted a grain mill, a brewery, and smelters to process the ores. California mission-style homes and buildings took their places among the low adobes in the booming towns. In 1889 the area's first university opened, New Mexico School of Mines. According to the 2000 census, Socorro's population was 8,877.

Getting There

Socorro is 76 miles south of Albuquerque and 194 miles north of El Paso. From I-25, take exit 147 or 150, which turns into California Street. Go west on Manzanares (one stoplight north of Spring St.) to the plaza. 110 Plaza; (575) 835–1193.

Wear and tear is evident on these handmade stool legs. If only they could talk.

Owl Bar owner Rowena Baca leans on her Brunswick-Balke-Collender bar and chats with the author.

Owl Bar

SAN ANTONIO

The first Hilton bar.
—Rowena Baca, owner

IMAGINE LUGGING A TWENTY-FIVE-FOOT MAHOGANY BAR down a gravel road for over two miles. In the heat of the blazing sun. Not by yourself, of course, but with the help of some of your crazy friends. How often would you have to stop, change grips, and go on? To do something like that, there's got to be one powerful thirst. But that's exactly what a group of motivated men did in the mid-1940s.

Rowena Baca, daughter of the Owl Bar's original owner, Frank Chavez, says, "A couple of years ago, a man came in and said that he and some others carried the bar down the street . . . about two miles. It took two days, but it got here in one piece."

In early 1945, when Frank Chavez came home to San Antonio, New Mexico, after serving in the U.S. Navy during the "Big War," he and his wife, Dee, opened a little bar in the grocery store operated by Dee's father, J. E. Miera. J. E. had been in business there since 1939, serving the needs of the local folks. Wanting to expand his business, Frank bought the bar and placed it along the north wall.

The Owl Bar, home of the famous OwlBurger, has remained a signature institution in San Antonio since 1945.

At the patrons' request, Frank put in a grill behind his bar and began cooking hamburgers. This was the birth of the world-famous OwlBurger, a mountainous green chile cheeseburger. Its recipe has remained unchanged since 1948.

Soon after the Owl Bar opened, it became the hangout of a handful of so-called prospectors who had recently moved into the tiny community. In actuality, these "prospectors" were the atomic scientists who had activated the famous Trinity Site detonation. This was the first test of the atomic bomb, soon to be used to end World War II.

Frank's daughter, Rowena, and her husband, Adolph Baca, operate the Owl Bar in much the same way Frank and Dee did. The story of this mahogany bar, in particular, is most interesting.

Before the turn of the twentieth century, a Norwegian immigrant, Augustus Halvorson (A. H.) Hilton, opened a boardinghouse/hotel for traveling salesmen and train passengers. Hilton ordered the 1880s Brunswick-Balke-Collender bar from Iowa and had it shipped to his San Antonio hotel. It was in this hotel where his son, Conrad, was a baggage carrier. (Conrad went on to create the world's largest hotel chain.) The bar sat in the A. H. Hilton Mercantile Store & Saloon until it burned down in 1945. They managed to save the front bar, but the back bar was lost.

Frank and Dee Baca bought the bar and moved it to its present location. Some time later, Rowena Baca doesn't know when, the standing bar was cut down "to where regular chairs fit nicely." Standing bars were designed for just that—standing—which makes finding the right height barstool difficult. Someone took care of that problem by lowering the bar.

The bar is a registered cultural property, which means it has been placed on the state register, deemed as being significant within a district.

This bar has been host to a who's who of elbows. For over 120 years, thousands of passersby have leaned (and then sat) here. They include many of New Mexico's rich and famous and people from around the world who have heard of this legendary spot. And who are they? Movie stars such as Neil Patrick Harris, Lee Remick, and Jane Fonda, businessman Ted Turner, producer Christopher Coppola, newsman (and New Mexican) Sam Donaldson, the band Megadeth, boxer Johnny Tapia, and countless governors and other politicos.

top: Age and dry desert days have split the mahogany capital.

left: The acanthus leaf design, seen in this capital and molding, was a classic signature of Brunwswick bars.

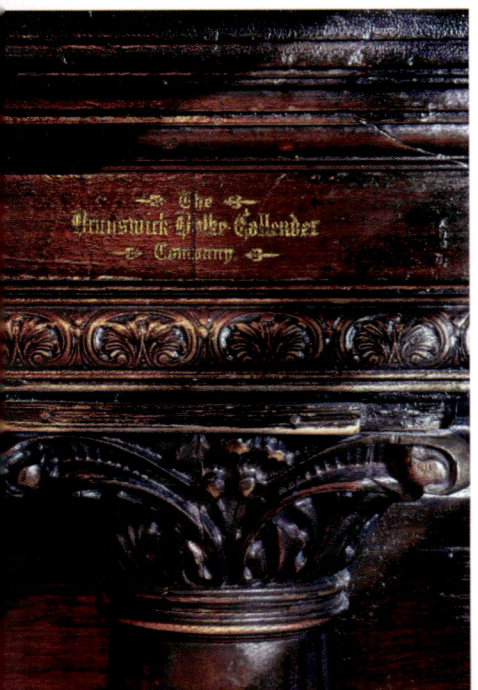

NEW MEXICO 98

History

San Antonio is an unincorporated community in Socorro County, New Mexico, roughly in the center of the state. The entire population of the county is around 18,000; the population of San Antonio is hard to pin down because the area is somewhat ill defined.

The town was named for the mission founded in 1629 by fray Antonio de Arteaga and fray Garcia de Francisco de Zúñiga. The U.S. Post Office was established in 1870.

San Antonio's base of income derives from agriculture, residents who work in Socorro and at White Sands Missile Range, and tourism. It is the gateway to the Bosque del Apache National Wildlife Refuge and the Trinity Site. I-25 runs along the west, the Rio Grande along the east, and the Burlington Northern Santa Fe Railway through it, maintaining a minimal yard. Conrad Hilton's name can still be seen ("C Hilton 1903") carved on the wall of what was once the schoolhouse, since then a mechanic's garage and now a barn.

Getting There

The Owl Bar is just east of I-25 on U.S. Highway 380, about 10 miles south of Socorro. Take exit 139 east, about a mile. Closed Sundays. P.O. Box 215; (505) 835–9946.

A flock of owls watch over the bar.

The Owl Bar's patrons include movie and television stars, politicos, cowboys, tourists, and even locals.

Most unusual, this blond mahogany bar once belonged to Al Capone.

Silver Dollar

TINNIE

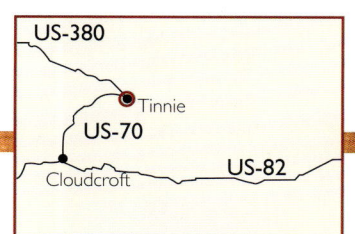

Billy the Kid may have slept here.
—Local resident

WITH ALL DUE RESPECT TO THE OLD WOODEN BARS ACROSS THE SOUTHWEST, the bar at the Silver Dollar is one of the best preserved in the area. The words *stunning* and *amazing* come to mind when first seeing the bar. *Handsome* and *well-crafted* are others. No matter which adjectives you choose, it's gorgeous.

A step into the former 1870 adobe and wood-frame general mercantile building is akin to stepping directly into history. Expanded over the years, this store and post office have been transformed into a steakhouse and saloon, purchased in 1959 by the oil tycoon Robert O. Anderson. Trophies of deer, Barbary sheep, pigs, bear, quail, and pheasant adorn the walls, as if watching the parade of history. Old photos of the building give black-and-white images of yesteryear. But color is the order of the day.

Between the dining room and billiard room sits the lounge, the magnificent Al Capone bar holding court over all the other antiques. This

In 1909 the Raymond family purchased this general store and post office. In 1959 Robert O. Anderson bought it and turned it into a steakhouse.

New Mexico artist and designer John Meigs restored the historic adobe and wood-frame building in 1959.

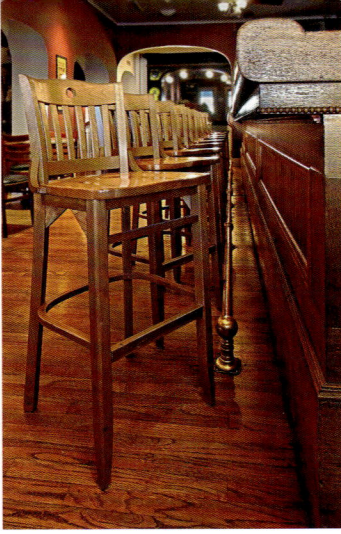

A solid brass foot rail offers support to patrons seated in the blond maple chairs lined up at the bar.

clockwise from bottom left: The back bar's attention to detail reveals true craftsmanship; smooth, clean lines are accentuated by beading that runs under the front bar counter; classic egg-and-dart molding rings the top of the column and the spandrel is decorated with a torch with acanthus leaves, egg-and-dart molding, and intricate beading; the first cash registers cost $100, were made of wood, and had no cash drawer.

original, handcrafted blond mahogany bar was owned by Chicago's main mobster until the 1940s. It sat in storage until Anderson discovered it and shipped it to southeastern New Mexico. He refinished the front and back counters but only by lightly sanding, then adding a protective sealant.

Setting off this twenty-five-foot standing bar are tiger wood columns on the back bar. Classic Greek egg-and-dart trim molding runs along the top of the Ionic columns and over the arches. Decorated with four torches and curlicues on each side, the columns set off the enormous mirrors. Although they are not original, the glass is antique.

A brass foot rail finishes off the look. Old but elegant. Capone knew class.

In the room but off to one side of the bar hangs another mirror. And not just any mirror. This one comes from a Chicago Harvey House and is reputed to be haunted. The image of a woman appears, as if approving the people who come to sit at Capone's bar. Or maybe she's waiting for someone to start up the wooden music box nearby. There are nine "records," heavy metal discs about twenty-four inches wide. This old gramophone still produces beautiful tones.

The antique mirror, acquired from a Harvey House in Chicago and reputed to be haunted, reflects the bar. It is said that the image of a young woman who seems to be searching for her lost lover can sometimes be seen in it.

History

Tinnie started out in the 1870s as Analla. Because some of the early settlers lived in caves, the town was also called Las Cuevas. In 1909 the Raymond family purchased a general store and post office and changed the name to Tinnie, after the family's daughter.

Tinnie is located in Lincoln County, where in 1878 Billy the Kid was jailed after taking part in the Lincoln County War, a conflict between ranchers and owners of the county's largest general store. Billy took the side of the English rancher John Tunstall, who had become a father figure to him. When a deputy killed Tunstall, Billy killed the deputy. After being arrested, he was promised a pardon by the governor, but it never came to fruition, and Billy escaped from the jail a few months later. He rode to Fort Sumner, where Sheriff Pat Garrett later killed him.

Today the Hondo Valley is home to small ranches and large fruit orchards. Tourism, artists, and produce keep the area alive.

In the room next to the bar stands this stained-glass fireplace, the perfect spot to warm hands on cold days.

An old cash register resides on the other side of the room, remembering days of nickel drinks.

Whose elbows have rested on this bar? More than likely Al Capone himself and his infamous associates. Other notables, most likely not involved in the same nefarious transactions as Capone, are producer Christopher Coppola, newsman Sam Donaldson, artists Peter Hurd and Michael Hurd, and businessman Robert O. Anderson.

Skiers, bikers, tourists, casino players, and hunters have stopped in and rested their elbows here. And let's not forget newlyweds. The Silver Dollar is event oriented, catering to weddings and family reunions. The Silver Dollar, currently owned by the Cattle Baron Restaurant Corporation, is a reminder of less complicated times.

Getting There

Tinnie, located in the Hondo River Valley, is on U.S. Highway 70, 43 miles west of Roswell, 28 miles east of Ruidoso, and 10 miles south of Lincoln. Tinnie Silver Dollar, Hondo; (575) 653–4425; www.tinniesilverdollar.com.

The silver dollar, the first dollar coin produced, was minted on October 15, 1794. The flowing hair design, shown here, was struck in 1794–95. The draped bust design was struck from 1795 to 1804.

Lodge reservations supervisor Beth Reese swaps stories over the handmade bar at the downstairs Red Dog Saloon.

Mobster Al Capone owned this upstairs bar. Now ghostly red-haired Rebecca watches over it.

The Lodge at Cloudcroft

CLOUDCROFT

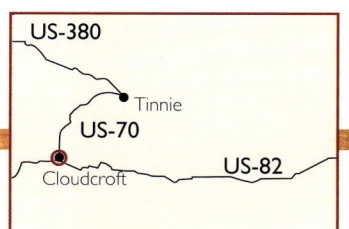

Home of the red-haired ghost.
—Saloon motto

HAVE YOU EVER HAD THE FEELING THAT SOMEBODY IS THERE, but no one is? If you're at the Lodge in Cloudcroft, it could be Rebecca, wearing a long dress, her red hair billowing and blue eyes flirting with you before she vanishes into thin mountain air.

Rebecca, the amorous ghost, was supposedly murdered by her jealous lumberjack boyfriend in the 1930s. Dozens of employees and guests have experienced her antics—moving ashtrays, making the phone ring in Room 101 (the Governor's Suite), causing flames to appear in the fireplace without benefit of logs or other fuel. She's mischievous but never harmful. And she makes having a drink at Rebecca's Lounge fun.

Burned to the ground in 1909, the Lodge was rebuilt within two years.

above: Rebecca is said to be searching for a lost lover.

below: Al Capone's picture is reflected in the back bar's mirror. If you sit in the right place, it feels like he's next to you.

top to bottom: The artisanship of this bar, which probably dates back to the 1880s, is undeniable. This fillet of delicate wood carvings lays across the top of the back bar. The scrollwork wraps around the column's edge; Victorian design was popular in 1880s bars, as it is on this capital. Handmade by Paul Hernandez, a 1930s hotel employee, this sixteen-foot bar in the Red Dog Saloon is made from locally grown pine and put together with pegs. It resides downstairs.

One reason the Lodge attracts visitors and locals alike is that there are two distinct lounges, with distinct bars. In the more sedate of the two, Rebecca's Lounge, stands an imposing, twenty-eight-foot mahogany bar, complete with a filled-in bullet hole. It was originally owned by the infamous Chicago mobster Al Capone.

"The front and back bar came together," says Beth Reese, the Lodge's reservations supervisor. She is quick to point out the intricate patterns in the molding across the top of the back bar. Its egg-and-dart pattern, first used by the Greeks, is said to signify never-ending cycles of life and death.

According to an article in the *Cloudcroft Daily News*, businessman R. O. Anderson, who leased the restaurant at the Lodge during the early 1970s, bought the bar from one of Al Capone's estates (perhaps the bar from Capone's Pony Inn on Van Buren Street in Chicago?), then trucked it here. The Brunswick-Balke-Collender back and front bars were most likely built around 1890, the heyday of bar building.

As for famous elbows resting on this bar, ordering drinks and telling stories, whose were they? Probably Capone and his Chicago associates. In fact, Capone's photo hangs on a wall opposite the bar mirror. If you sit in the right place, it appears that he's sitting next to you.

A frequent visitor from southeastern New Mexico says he stops by whenever he's in town, just to sit and soak in the quiet and the welcome of the Lodge. If he went downstairs, however, he would find quite a different atmosphere.

The Red Dog Saloon, open for parties such as wedding receptions and dining events, hosts live music a few times a year. Located on a lower level, the Red Dog wooden bar was built by Paul Hernandez, a hotel employee, in the 1930s. This sixteen-foot bar is made from locally grown pine and put together with pegs. Many people have carved their names on the top, adding to the bar's character.

Named after a big red dachshund–basset hound cross who belonged to a former Lodge owner, the Red Dog Saloon is also called the Trestle Room. The rustic pine front and back bars grace one entire wall and have felt their share of celebrities' elbows. "Rebecca used to dance here a lot," says Reese. She wasn't clear if that was before or after Rebecca became a ghost.

Gilbert Roland, Judy Garland, and Clark Gable, plus state governors and other notables, have lifted a few at this incredible bar.

"We're trying to get locals to come in and relive the feel of the Red Dog," reports Reese. It was known as a rowdy place at one point, where everybody came to be seen and enjoy themselves.

"It's a nice ol' bar," Reese says, a wistful smile crossing her face. Perhaps in a previous incarnation she was red-haired.

Originally built in 1899 by the Alamogordo and Sacramento Railway, the Lodge burned to the ground in 1909. But like the mythical Phoenix, it was resurrected out of the ashes to return bigger and better two years later.

History

Charles Bishop Eddy and his brother, John Arthur Eddy, organized the El Paso and Northeastern Railrway to include the new town of Alamogordo. They intended to continue the rail line to White Oaks and beyond but needed a supply of timber. In 1898 the brothers sent a survey crew into the Sacramento Mountains to determine if building a supply line through the forest was feasible. The crew sent word that a line was possible and that the area would attract visitors. The name Cloudcroft (pasture for clouds) was suggested and stuck. The railroad line arrived in Cloudcroft in early 1900, and by June of that year the train depot was completed.

Known as a summer retreat from the desert heat, Cloudcroft is also a winter playground, offering the southernmost ski lift in the lower 48. Today's population of just under 800 is bolstered by a year-round tourist trade.

Getting there

From Alamogordo, take U.S. Highway 82 east, 19 miles. The Lodge is located at 1 Corona Place; (800) 395–6343; www.thelodgeresort.com.

The brass foot rail is supported by brass gryphons.

Over the past eighty years people have carved their names into the Red Dog Saloon's bar and the handmade stools.

Located upstairs in the lobby, Rebecca's image is etched in glass.

This Brunswick-Balke-Collender bar was freighted from Hillsborough, New Mexico, after surviving travel from Iowa.

Buckhorn Saloon

PINOS ALTOS

Horse-drawn wagons brought the bar.
—Saloon brochure

THE WOODEN PLANK FLOORS CREAK WHEN PEOPLE WALK into the Buckhorn. That's all right, because not only is the floor old, but the building is too. Built in 1865, the Buckhorn is one of six original buildings dating to the 1860s, when Pinos Altos was established. But this is the only saloon building in town dating back that far. During the boom years seven drinking establishments served the miners, prospectors, and cowboys who wandered through.

The saloon itself is not a big room, so the magnificent Brunswick-Balke-Collender bar takes up half of the area. Freighted in from Hillsborough, New Mexico, on horse-drawn wagons in 1897, the front and back bars found a home at the Buckhorn. They have sat there ever since. A rarity, the mirror is original, as is the brass foot rail.

Even the potbelly stove, greeting customers at the door, has graced the Buckhorn for over one hundred years. The coal oil lanterns and a roaring fireplace add a touch of Old West ambience to the building, its eighteen-inch-thick adobe walls keeping the heat in or the cold out. Since Pinos Altos (Spanish for "tall pines") nestles up to the base of the Mogollon Mountains,

Built in 1865, the Buckhorn is constructed with eighteen-inch-thick adobe walls and hand-hewn support timbers.

This was one of the first electric lights to hang on each side of the back bar.

A kerosene light that has been converted to electricity is suspended from the wooden ceiling. Trophies of indigenous animals watch over the bar.

Indian Joe, a regular at the bar, waits for tips.

Pinos Altos sits in the mountains, and this parlor stove is well used.

hunting is a natural sport in the area. Deer and bison trophies, along with pronghorn sheep, watch over the patrons.

Other than miners, prospectors, and cowboys from the turn of the twentieth century, whose elbows have rested on this bar? "Lots of tourists and locals, such as the Red Hat Society," says the manager. And celebrities: actors Keanu Reeves, Woody Harrelson, Charlize Theron, and Hank Thompson. The list goes on. And while admittedly Pinos Altos is not on a major highway, or close to one, many intrepid types find themselves enjoying a glass or two at the Buckhorn.

The Buckhorn has operated as a steakhouse and saloon since the early 1960s. Previously, it was a one-room saloon—nice and cozy, perfect for cold winter days. Now it's still cozy, just a bit roomier.

History

Three prospectors fresh from the California goldfields stopped in 1860 at the Bear Creek for a drink of water. What they found was gold. Word naturally got out, and Birchville, later named Pinos Altos, boomed. Roy Bean operated a general store here with his brother, Sam, before moving west to Texas. Pinos Altos was home to a Hearst (of newspaper fame) gold mine.

In the 1880s and 1890s the population hovered at 9,000, and the town had a few churches, a school, a general mercantile, and other establishments. As the town grew, it was subject to frequent raids by the Apache Indians who lived in the Mogollon Mountains. In fact, the oldest house—the McDonald Cabin, built about 1851, around the corner from the Buckhorn on Spring Street—still sports a few arrow holes, attesting to some wild and woolly times.

On September 27, 1861, some five hundred Apaches, led by Cochise and Mangas Coloradas,

Left to right: An eagle perches on top of the back bar. Note the dentils and scrollwork carvings; Debbie DeCamp watches over the Buckhorn, here enjoying the view from the balcony; a brass foot rail anchors the mahogany bar; in 1860 gold was discovered in Bear Creek near Birchville, present-day Pinos Altos (Tall Pines).

attacked Pinos Altos. The miners killed more than a dozen Indians, and the Apaches killed three miners. A few months later forty miners were killed after being distracted by attractive Indian women whom Mangas Coloradas had placed strategically near town. The graves of a few of these victims are located in the cemetery next to the Methodist-Episcopal church.

Fortunately, today much more peaceful activities are the norm, especially during the summer. Arts and crafts fairs, outdoor concerts, and melodramas abound during the warm weather.

Getting There

Pinos Altos is 6 miles north of Silver City. From I-25, take exit 63 west on Highway 152, 67 miles, to Highway 15. Or on I-10, from Deming, travel north on Highway 180 to Highway 15; take Highway 15 at Silver City, and travel north to Pinos Altos. In town the streets can be muddy in summer monsoons and frozen during the winter. The Buckhorn is on Main Street, across from the Pinos Altos Museum; (575) 538–9911; buckhornsaloonandoperahouse.com.

This 1880s thirty-foot oak and walnut Imperial bar was originally in the Drake Hotel in Chicago. It was designed by Charles Eastlake, whose style was popular in England and America in the late 1800s.

The Ferdinand Bar, hand carved with gilded cherubs and columns, sits in the Isabela Ballroom.

Double Eagle

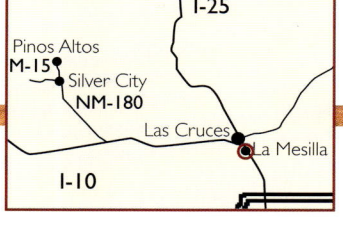

LA MESILLA

The crown jewel of Old Mesilla.
—Saloon motto

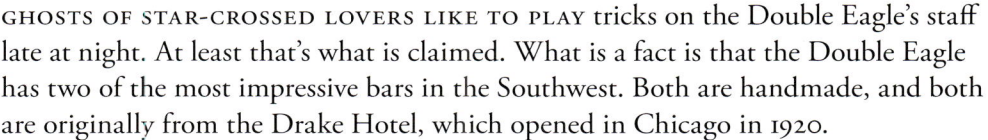

GHOSTS OF STAR-CROSSED LOVERS LIKE TO PLAY tricks on the Double Eagle's staff late at night. At least that's what is claimed. What is a fact is that the Double Eagle has two of the most impressive bars in the Southwest. Both are handmade, and both are originally from the Drake Hotel, which opened in Chicago in 1920.

When oil tycoon Robert O. Anderson bought the Double Eagle restaurant in the 1970s, he purchased these two bars and shipped them to La Mesilla. Whatever he paid for them was a bargain. The thirty-foot hand-carved oak and walnut Eastlake-style bar, framed with four gold-leafed Corinthian columns, greets guests at the entry. Glittering light spreads over antique Americana paintings. A gilded French Baccarat crystal chandelier hangs from the pressed tin ceiling.

"We have a phenomenal collection of art," says the Double Eagle's current owner, Buddy Ritter. While the art is impressive, it is the wooden

Classic French Baccarat chandeliers, measuring seven feet by three feet, light the Imperial Bar.

The Double Eagle, built of sturdy adobe in the 1840s, is the oldest structure on the La Mesilla Plaza.

above: Fine craftsmanship such as this peg cover detail enhances this oak Imperial bar.

giving it the reverence it deserves. Near the bottom of the front bar is a brass foot rail originally from La Mesilla's former Billy the Kid Saloon.

"I don't know where you'd find another bar like this," says Ritter. The workmanship is astounding, and it is generally assumed that the bar is custom made, by hand, of course.

In the back of the restaurant, in the Isabela Ballroom, sits the Ferdinand Bar. Made of red oak, it measures about thirteen feet. Also custom made, this 1890s bar was installed in the Double Eagle in the early 1970s. Gilded cherubs and four grooved Corinthian columns rest on marble bases on the back bar. The columns support an arch with ten floral light fixtures.

The Isabela Ballroom is used for special events, such as wedding receptions and corporate functions. The gilded gold ceiling is reminiscent of days past, when Confederate officers held dances here.

above top: French floral Corones light the back bar. Each contains twenty-three lighted brass flowers.

above bottom: Ten of the lights have blue Lalique crystal rosette shades.

masterpiece, the Imperial Bar, as it is referred to by the staff, that takes one's breath away. Original top mirrors in the back bar reflect light cast by two Imperial French floral Corones, each five feet tall with twenty-three lighted brass flowers. The Lalique shades date from the 1890s.

The Imperial Bar is located directly to the left of the entryway. Thirty feet is long for a bar, and this one fits the space nicely. At some point during its life, the front bar's top was damaged, and pieces from a gym floor in Deming, New Mexico, replaced it. The staff keeps the bar highly polished,

An acanthus leaf design in gold gilding sets off the top of this Corinthian column.

NEW MEXICO 114

clockwise from left: Dentil ornamentation decorates the Ferdinand's cornice molding; cherubs are surrounded by egg-and-dart molding; even the bottom of the front bar's base shows high craftsmanship.

The building itself is the oldest on La Mesilla's historic plaza, dating back more than 150 years. Declared a National Landmark, the building is also listed on the National Register of Historic Places. It started out as a home and has witnessed the beginning of the Mexican-American War of 1846; the confirmation of the Gadsden Purchase on the plaza on December 30, 1853; the Secessionist Convention declaration of La Mesilla as the capital of Arizona Territory in 1861; and, of course, Billy the Kid's 1881 escape from jail, which was located a few doors down the block. The Kid probably ran into this building to hide, or at least sprinted past.

Since both bars came from the Drake Hotel in Chicago, more than likely many notable elbows have rested on them, hoisting a few to good times. In Chicago these may have included the elbows of Winston Churchill, Elizabeth Taylor, Judy Garland, Hugh Hefner, and Frank Sinatra. Paul Newman once visited, as did Ted Turner and Jane Fonda, as well as many tourists and regulars.

"This bar is the one single women come to," says Ritter. "They feel comfortable here, and it speaks awfully well of this bar."

History—Double Eagle

This adobe home was built during the boom time for La Mesilla in the 1840s and is the oldest building in

top: A French crystal chandelier hangs in front of the Ferdinand Bar in the Isabela Ballroom.

bottom: Intricate oak supports hold up the counter of the Ferdinand Bar. Note the beading.

Gold gilded carvings sit at the center top of the Imperial Bar.

This antique chandelier hangs in the middle of the Imperial Bar.

Historic Old Mesilla. It was a private residence until the 1950s, when it was abandoned for a time, then used as a cotton warehouse. It became a series of shops until 1972. It was then purchased by Robert O. Anderson, who hired the internationally known artist and designer John Meigs to collect the museum-quality antiques, paintings, sculptures, woodwork, and other decorative items, making the Double Eagle unique. A fifth-generation resident of La Mesilla, Buddy Ritter, refitted the building in 1984 with modern heating and air-conditioning and enclosed a patio.

The name "Double Eagle" was taken from a U.S. gold coin minted in the 1850s. The $10 piece was known as the Eagle and the $20 piece as the Double Eagle.

History—La Mesilla

In 1852 La Mesilla was home to 700 settlers. The territorial legislature claimed the entire strip of what is now the southern third of New Mexico and Arizona, extending 800 miles from Texas to the

Colorado River. They named it Doña Ana County, and La Mesilla became the county seat.

By 1860 La Mesilla was home to 3,000 people. A major stopover for the Butterfield Overland Stageline, La Mesilla was the center of freighting, farming, and mercantile and was the largest town between San Diego and San Antonio. However, this area turned pro-Confederacy and became the capital of the Arizona Territory of the Confederate States in 1861. The flag flew for thirteen months. When it became obvious that the Confederacy would not be victorious, the territory was again placed in U.S. hands, and Union soldiers were "welcomed" into town, especially with the government contracts they brought.

The town continued to grow until 1881, when the railroad bypassed it in favor of Las Cruces, 5 miles away. Today La Mesilla is a lively, thriving community filled with multigenerational families and artists.

Getting There

From I-10, take exit 140 west onto Avenida de Mesilla, which becomes Highway 28. Travel south 1 mile to Calle de Santiago. From I-25, take I-10 west to La Mesilla, exit 140, then south 1 mile on Highway 28 to Calle de Santiago. Turn west two blocks to the plaza. Double Eagle Restaurant faces the plaza on the east side. (575) 523–6700; www.double-eagle-mesilla.com.

Minted in the 1850s, the $10 gold coin was known as the Eagle, and the $20 gold coin was the Double Eagle.

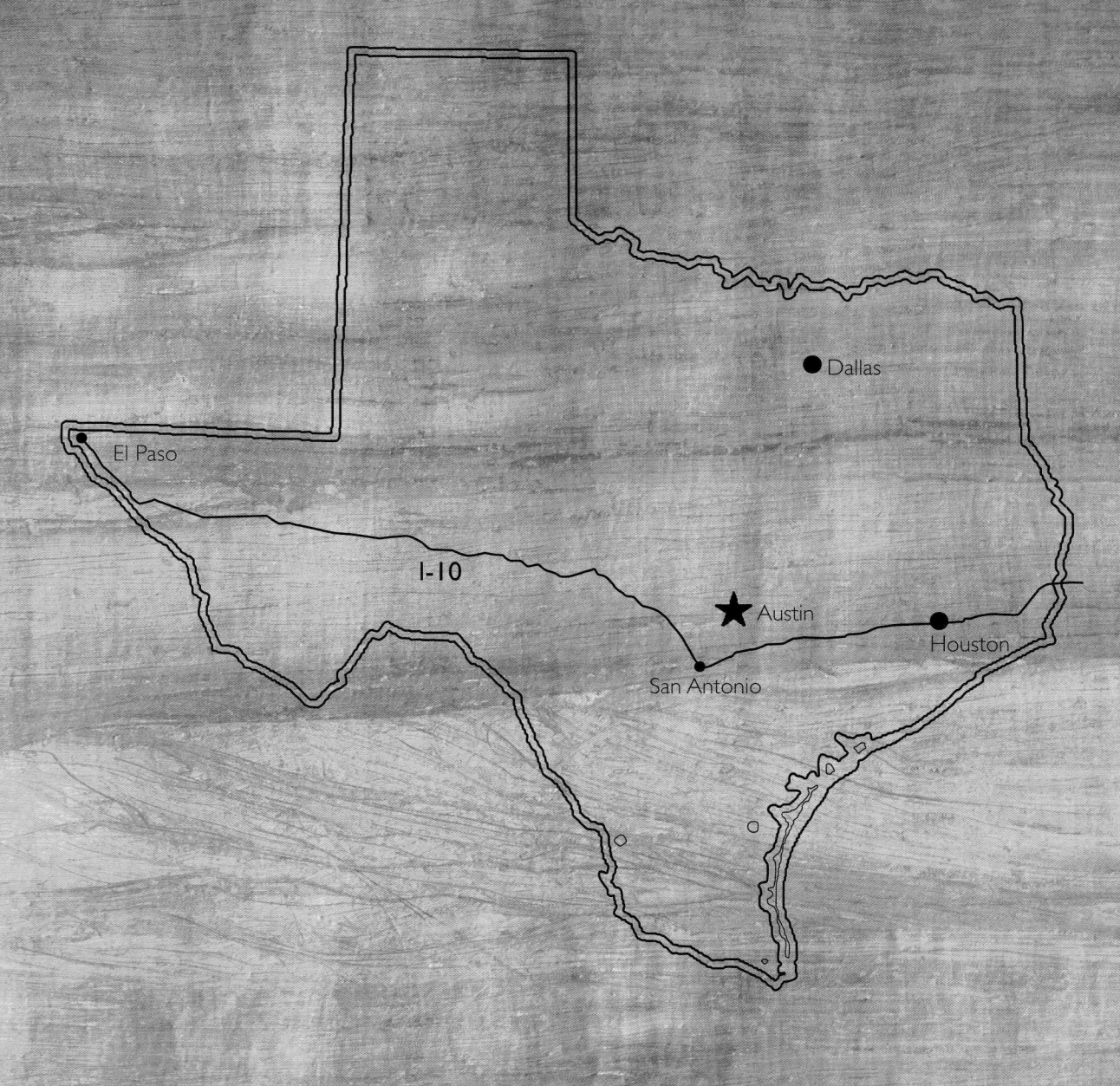

Texas

Locals and tourists, old and young, mingle at Rosa's Cantina.

Rosa's Cantina

EL PASO

Out in the West Texas town of El Paso . . .
—Marty Robbins, songwriter

"NIGHTTIME WOULD FIND ME IN ROSA'S CANTINA . . . Music would play and Feleena would whirl."

Makes you want to sing along, doesn't it? Images of cowboys, horses, whiskey, smoky barrooms, and painted ladies all dance in your head. And it happens right here at Rosa's.

Now, Rosa's Cantina doesn't date from the 1800s, as the legendary song would lead us to believe. But it is pretty famous. Claims have been made that Marty Robbins was inspired by this cantina situated at the edge of El Paso. In fact, it's so "edgy" that New Mexico's border is within a stone's throw of the front door. Sunland Park Racetrack is located across the street and north just a bit—a bit enough to be in New Mexico.

Standing in Rosa's doorway, it's easy to get lost in Robbins's song "El Paso," his famous story of love gone wrong. Hills *do* overlook the cantina, and the "badlands of New Mexico" are just over those hills. It's easy to envision cowboys "as wild as the West Texas wind" come riding up to the hitchin' rail, then strolling in with visions of beer and señoritas in mind. It's easy to be swept back to days when music would whirl just like Feleena.

Rosa's Cantina is in Texas, but New Mexico is right across the street.

top: A hard polish luster finishes off this horseshoe-shaped tiger and red oak bar.

bottom: Red oak flooring makes a dandy bar top.

Robbins's family explains on Marty's official website why he wrote "El Paso." Robbins grew up in Phoenix and early in his music career had traveled to Nashville, Tennessee, to record and write some songs. He and his family were on their way home when they drove through El Paso. The interstate system was just an idea at this time, so Doniphan Drive was a main thoroughfare to get to Phoenix, and of course the Robbinses drove past Rosa's Cantina.

Looking around, Robbins thought the hills were in Mexico. When he was corrected—the hills are actually in *New Mexico*—he was so taken with the stark beauty of the area and the name of the bar that inspiration struck, and as he rode in the car he wrote the song. By the time they reached Deming, New Mexico, about two hours from El Paso, he had finished it.

Inspired by the famous song, which sits at number five on the all-time favorite country music chart, Rosa's Cantina welcomes everyone. Locals, some of whom are cowboys, horse racing enthusiasts, sports fanatics, tourists, and musicians, come galloping up to the cantina now, tethering their rides with a click of a lock. Rosa's Cantina is one big room with two doors—a restaurant door and a cantina door. Don't be fooled.

They open into the same place. Just as in the old days, both English and Spanish flow freely, often in the same sentence. And everybody knows what is being said.

A grand horseshoe-shaped bar takes up half of the Cantina. Its owner, Oscar Lopez, says it's their trademark. Made of tiger oak and red oak flooring, its glassy shine comes from a hard polish luster. A pool table and jukebox along with red-checkered-cloth covered tables finish off the inside of the Cantina. The walls sport old vinyl LPs: Sunny and the Sunliners, Freddy Fender, and, of course, Marty Robbins. In fact, there are a couple of signed photos of Marty hanging around. "El Paso" was the first country song ever to win a Grammy Award.

Originally opened in the late 1920s as Los Tigres, the business was purchased by Anita and Roberto Zubia in 1957 and renamed Rosa's Cantina. According to a regular customer, there's "so much love in this place" that old and young people comingle. She says there's "one type of everybody in here"—from well-employed corporate chiefs to the not-so-well-employed.

But there is always a catch to being a regular in a famous bar. According to this customer, "When tourists come in, you gotta listen to *that* song." She sighs and rolls her eyes. "So we sit and listen." In fact, an older couple on their way from Florida had stopped by, she said, and put money in the jukebox for *that* song. When it was over, the man revealed that he had played in a band with Marty Robbins several years ago, and he had always wanted to see Rosa's Cantina. Possibly the most unusual guest was a gentleman from Canada who rode horseback over two thousand miles just to see Rosa's Cantina.

Oscar Lopez says his family grew up and worked near the smelter on El Paso's west side. He says that with so much history here, in terms of both family and history, when it came on the market he couldn't pass up the chance to buy it. "Rosa's Cantina brought El Paso to the map fifty years ago [with the song], and we're hoping to bring Rosa's back to El Paso." While the world knows of Rosa's Cantina, apparently much of El Paso doesn't. Oscar Lopez intends to change that, one patron at a time.

The horseshoe bar shimmers in the neon beer lights. And who knows who whirls late at night when the bar is closed? Could it be Feleena and her cowboy?

History

Originally known as Franklin, El Paso officially became part of the United States when Texas joined the Union in 1845. The Texas Republic wanted a slice of the Santa Fe Trail trade, and the Treaty of Guadalupe Hidalgo effectively made the settlements on the north bank of the Rio Grande a formal American settlement, separate from old El Paso del Norte (today's Juárez, Mexico). Early in the Mexican-American War (1846–48), the Battle of El Brazito, near Las Cruces, was fought by Missouri volunteers and led by Col. Alexander William Doniphan, for whom Doniphan Drive is named.

The first military post, Fort Bliss, was established along the American side of the river in 1849 to protect the route to the goldfields farther west. Fort Bliss was sited at various locations in the area before it arrived at its permanent location.

Although El Paso leaned toward the Confederacy side during the Civil War, it was not much affected by the war. Incorporated in 1873 and encompassing the area communities along the river (Magoffinsville, Concordia, Hart's Mill), El Paso grew in 1881 with the arrival of the railroad. Business boomed. It earned the nickname "Six Shooter Capital" because of its lawlessness, with saloons, dance halls, gambling establishments, and "houses of ill-repute" up and down the main streets. The "Four Dead in Five Seconds Gunfight" took place on April 14, 1881. A newly hired marshal shot and killed the former town marshal, an area rancher and known cattle rustler, a constable, and an innocent bystander running for cover.

Things have calmed down quite a bit since then. Fort Bliss has become a major training and missile defense center. The University of Texas at El Paso is an outstanding four-year university, and retail and banking business still booms. Today's population totals over 606,000.

Getting There

From I-10 in El Paso, take exit 13 west onto Sunland Park. Go two blocks and turn south (left) onto Doniphan. Rosa's Cantina is at the end of Doniphan; 3454 Doniphan Drive; (915) 479-0825.

A cow skull watches over the Texas state flag.

Mike and Melody Groves on the road.